Pocketguide to WESTERN HATCHES

Dave Hughes

HEADWATER BOOKS

STACKPOLE BOOKS

STACKPOLE BOOKS
The Globe Pequot Publishing Group, Inc.
64 South Main Street
Essex, CT 06426
www.globepequot.com

Distributed by NATIONAL BOOK NETWORK

Printed in India

First edition

Cover design by Tracy Patterson.
Photos by the author except where noted.
Illustrations by Richard Bunse.

Cataloging-in-Publication data is on file with the Library of Congress

ISBN 978-0-8117-0736-7

Contents

Acknowledgments

I would first like to thank the late Ernest Schwiebert. His book *Nymphs* was the first to inspire me to go out to a stream, turn over submerged rocks, and get exposed to all the mysteries in the aquatic world where trout make most of their living by eating insects.

Next I'd like to thank Professor Norman Anderson, who allowed me to audit his aquatic entomology class at Oregon State University. He explained to me many of those mysteries about the world of insects and trout, but also revealed that there were a lot more to solve, or attempt to.

I'd like to thank Rick Hafele, young lab assistant to Norm Anderson in that aquatic entomology class, for more years of collaboration and friendship than either of us would care to count, including a couple of coauthored books. I still pester Rick with questions whenever we go fishing together, which is still often.

I owe more thanks than I can calculate to Jim Schollmeyer, as much for quiet sharing of trout streams as for advice about taking photos of aquatic insects. Many of the hatches recorded in this book were fished with Jim. Some of the photographs of insects are his. All of the others were taken under his instructions.

I'm not sure whether I owe Richard Bunse more for his fine illustrations in this book and many others, or for his thoughtful observations on the way life should be lived. He's the one I turn to when I need a Magical Mystery Tour to sort something out . . . those tours invariably end in some place where trout can be found.

I'd like to thank Jay Nichols, who had the idea for this book and asked me to write it. In an earlier instar he was my editor at *Fly Fisherman* magazine. Now he is an editor at Stackpole Books.

He was also my guide on a hectic trip fishing Pennsylvania trout streams.

Of course, I must thank my wife, fishing writer Masako Tani, for propelling me out to trout waters all over the world. Long ago I had to explain to her the old saying that curiosity will kill a cat. She still loves to fish and explore waters near and far, and it hasn't killed her yet.

I'd like to express special thanks to Tracy Peterson, professional tier, guide, and author, for tying the flies for this book while I recovered from cataract surgery, so much more gracefully than I could have ever done it anyway.

Finally, I'd like to thank my daughter Kosumo. I spoiled her with a Mac computer ahead of the rest of her school classmates, and also well ahead of my own switch from the constant disasters of PCs. It turned out to be the best investment I ever made. Now, when I need help with the new computer, I merely yelp for her.

PART ONE

Notes on Western Hatches

1 Using This Guide

It's necessary to clarify the term *hatch* as it's used in fly fishing. For the purpose of this book, *a hatch is defined as a specific stage of any food form that is abundant and available and therefore fed on selectively by trout*. The food might be an aquatic insect such as a mayfly in its nymph, emerger, dun, or spinner stage, or a caddisfly in its larva, pupa, adult, or egg-laying stage. It might also be a terrestrial insect falling to the water in sufficient numbers to cause trout to focus on it, or an overwhelming abundance of a particular crustacean in aquatic plant beds. Some of these are true *hatches*, in which insects emerge from their nymph or pupal stage. Some are not. But all can cause trout to feed selectively and therefore become the one thing that you must match to succeed in catching those trout at that moment.

Selective feeding is the criteria for a hatch in this book. If trout focus on a specific stage of a single food form, and in doing so turn away from everything else and refuse to take any fly that fails to look like it, you need to focus on it yourself, in that old process that we commonly call *matching the hatch*, whether it's an actual hatch or not. You should always follow a logical set of steps in matching any hatch, whether consciously or, as you become more experienced, subconsciously.

1. Observe trout, whether on the surface, in the mid-depths, or along the bottom, and determine that they're feeding selectively. If active trout refuse the first flies you show them, back away and observe what they're doing. They won't often reject generic fly patterns unless they're focused on something specific.

The criteria for a *hatch* in this book is that a specific stage of an insect, or any other trout food form, causes selective feeding. When a trout feeds only on one stage of a single species, and ignores everything that doesn't look like it, then you must match it to have any hope of catching that trout.

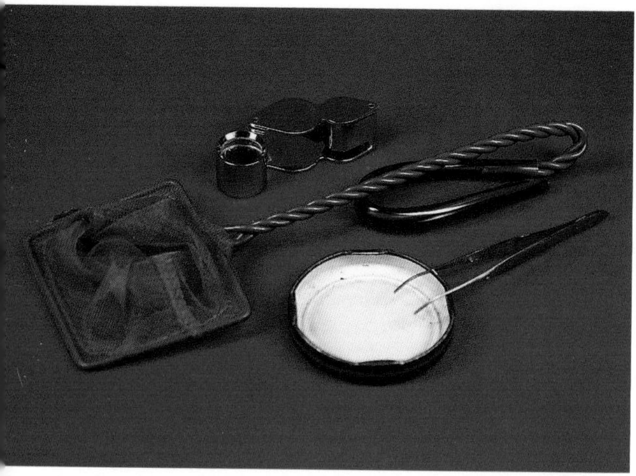

A small number of collecting aids will enable you to get that critical close look at an insect. An aquarium net will let you lift insects from the surface or catch them in the air. A small hand glass, no more than 5X magnification, will let you compare the natural to the descriptions in this book. A pair of tweezers will help you handle small and fragile insects. A pickle jar lid, white inside, can be filled with water, and will help you observe natural nymphs and larvae.

2. Capture a specimen of whatever they're eating. You don't need to carry an entomologist's long-handled net. But you will improve your observation abilities, and therefore your angling skills, if you carry a small aquarium net along with a pocket magnifying glass. Add a pair of tweezers, plus the white lid from a pickle or relish jar in which to place aquatic specimens, and you'll have all you'll ever need without giving away much space in your vest pockets.

3. Observe the insect or other food form closely, paying particular attention to its size, shape, and color. Note the characteristics that will enable you to recognize it: the number of tails, shape of the body and wings, length of antennae, and any other features.

4. Compare the insect you've captured to the photos in this book, and to the lists of key features. Most often you'll be able to find the right insect without any trouble. But it's very important to know that only the most important and widespread Western hatches are included in this book. When trout feed selectively, it will usually be on something that is listed here. But it's impossible to encompass them all. If your specimen doesn't have precisely the same characteristics as an insect in the book, but its size, form, and color are the same as one you've found here, match it with the fly that looks most like it. It's a little-known secret that trout never bother to identify the species of insects or anything else before eating them.

5. Note the type of habitat in which you've found trout feeding selectively. This will inform you about what *style* of imitation will work best and the way you should fish it. For example, if the insect is hatching in a riffle, you'll need a dry fly with hackle for flotation, and you'll want to fish it with an upstream presentation. If it's hatching on a flat, you'll need less hackle and a more exact silhouette of the natural, and you'll need to fish it on a cross-stream or downstream presentation to avoid spooking the trout with your line and leader.

6. Notice the manner of the insect's emergence: does it crawl out on streamside rocks or emerge out in open water, perhaps struggling in the surface film? At this step, watch riseforms as trout feed on the insect, and observe which stage they might be taking. I often carry small binoculars to follow floating insects. If I see a fleet of mayfly duns all drifting safely through a pod of rising trout, without any ever disappearing, then I know I need to imitate emergers.

7. Select a fly pattern to imitate the stage of the insect or other food form that you've determined trout are taking selectively. The best fly might be a nymph, an emerger, a dry fly, perhaps a wet fly, sometimes even a streamer. Whatever it is, you've based your selection on careful observation of first the trout, second

The habitat in which you find an insect hatching and being fed upon selectively by trout will inform your fly pattern selection. If the water is rough, you'll want a hackled pattern because flotation is just as important as imitation. If the water is smooth, you'll want a more imitative pattern and will not need hackle to float the fly.

what the trout are taking, and third the water type in which they're taking it.

8. Choose your rigging and your presentation method based on the behavior of the natural on which the trout are feeding. If it's an adult floating without disturbance on the water, rig with a leader and tippet appropriate for the water, and present the fly with a drag-free drift. If it's a damselfly nymph migrating toward the edges of a lake or pond, rig to fish the nymph shallow with a very slow retrieve.

9. If fish refuse your chosen fly and method, don't frantically change flies. Instead, check your initial observations. See if the trout are taking what you think they are, and make sure you've imitated the right stage of the insect at the correct level in the water column or on top of it. Check your rigging, and make sure it's suited to the fly you're using and the water where you're using it. If your observations are correct, it's more common to change your luck by adding three feet of fine tippet than it is by switching to yet another imitative dry fly.

These steps in matching a hatch quickly become intuitive. You don't frisk yourself and find a cheat-sheet at streamside, check off the steps as if you were a pilot preparing for takeoff. You simply observe the trout, get a look at what they're taking, match it, rig, and present the fly in the way the natural might move in front of the trout. If it doesn't work, you look things over again, adjust whatever you might have gotten wrong, or more likely, adjust to whatever has changed since you made your first set of observations. Trout will focus on one stage of an insect for a while, and you'll catch them very well. Then they'll abruptly decide to focus their feeding on another stage or some other insect. If you fail to notice the change, you'll soon discover that you're not catching anything. Constant awareness of what is happening around you will keep you constantly and pleasantly engaged with trout.

2 The Wide Variety of Western Waters

The West, in terms of both landscape and species lists, begins roughly along the line of the eastern front of the Rocky Mountains. This is not arbitrary; the vast grasslands of the Great Plains are a natural barrier to migration, and therefore distribution, of many species, especially aquatic insects.

From north to south, a line of states and a Canadian province form the biological dividing line between the West and the Midwest and East: Saskatchewan, North Dakota, South Dakota, Nebraska, Kansas, Oklahoma, and Texas. Western and Eastern aquatic insect species lists are roughly divided by this region. Trout waters in the Great Plains are as likely to have Midwestern, Eastern, or Western hatches, so a lot of what is written in this book applies in them. You'll find many *Western hatches* in those central states and provinces, including Manitoba, Canada. When you do, you'll discover trout feeding on them just as they do farther west, and you should use the same dressings to match them and the same methods to present those flies.

DEFINING WESTERN WATERS

Our Western geography is so diverse that describing trout waters in the West means defining trout waters anywhere and everywhere. But some description is worth pursuing because many aquatic insects live in specific water types, and even those that hatch on a wide variety of water types must be imitated with different flies on the separate types or your results might not be satisfying.

As a brief example, you might fish a Western Green Drake emergence on a tumbling headwater stream and the same insect

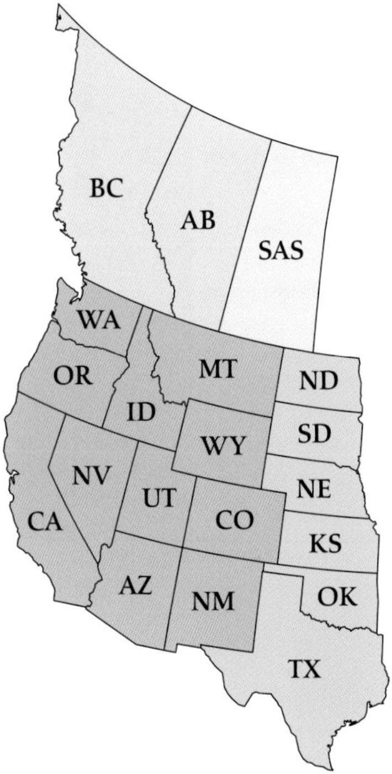

Western States and Provinces: British Columbia, Alberta, Washington, Idaho, Montana, Oregon, Wyoming, California, Nevada, Utah, Colorado, Arizona, New Mexico.

Dividing States and Provinces: Saskatchewan, North Dakota, South Dakota, Nebraska, Kansas, Oklahoma, Texas.

on the smooth waters of the Henrys Fork of the Snake River. You'd be smart to use a hackled dry fly to match the insect on the mountain stream, because it would float there. But the same pattern would be viewed with disdain by trout on the Henrys Fork. And the low-floating imitation that would con picky trout on smooth and heavily-fished water would not float well on the more boisterous small stream.

You might encounter the same Blue-Winged Olive hatch on a rough headwater stream or on some of the smoothest and most heavily fished waters in the West, but you need to treat it differently on the two water types. The imitation that would float on the fast little stream would not fool trout on the flats of the larger river. The imitation that would take trout there might not even float on the headwater stream. You also need to change your tactics: On the small stream, you would fish upstream, and do fine. But on the flats of a larger river, you'd need to use a cross-stream reach cast or downstream wiggle cast to have a hope of catching many trout.

A freestone mountain stream has more plunge pools than any other water type. Trout hold wherever the water is slow enough, and dug deep enough, for them to find some shelter from currents and protection from predators. Food is varied, and trout will rarely be selective.

Freestone mountain and headwater creeks. These have rocky bottoms and swift currents interrupted by plunge pools carved to minor depths. They have the greatest diversity of aquatic insects and the fewest concentrated hatches. Different types of terrestrial insects also constantly fall to the surface of their small runs, glides, and pools. A trout has little time to examine a bit of food, or a fly, before the current either whisks it away or another trout beats it to it. Small-stream trout cannot afford to be picky. They are least likely to become selective. It's wise to fish such water with searching flies such as the Royal Wulff or Elk Hair Caddis. If you notice an insect in abundance, then match it as nearly as you can, but be sure your dry-fly imitation has plenty of flotation, or you'll find it less effective than a less imitative fly that floats well.

Foothill trout streams often have classic pools. Though they offer trout lots of variety, in terms of food forms, they also have concentrated emergences and falls of spinners and terrestrials. Trout often become selective, and you need to match what's happening to be more successful.

Freestone foothill and valley streams. These have gradients that are not as steep as those of mountain creeks. They're characterized by the riffle/run/pool structure that fly fishers consider classic. Their pools tend to be larger than those in mountain streams, and their trout tend to take territories where the currents erode the deepest depths. Their bottoms vary from pebbles through cobble to boulders. They have a wide diversity of aquatic insect hatches and falls of terrestrials, but in the slower water types one insect often dominates others, and trout become selective to it. When they do, select your imitation by the type of water over which you'll fish it. If trout are rising mostly in riffles or runs, use a hackled fly. If they're feeding on the smoother water of pools, use a more accurate imitation with less flotation.

Large Western trout rivers have all of their different water types—riffles, runs, pools, and flats—in big and somewhat separate sections. Insects in the various water types tend to be homogenous and therefore often hatch in concentrated numbers over distinct periods of time. When such a hatch is happening, you need to match it with a pattern chosen for the water type in which the trout are feeding. You will often cast over a pod of trout and wear it out after catching a few. Move upstream or down to a similar stretch of water, and you're likely to find another pod of undisturbed trout.

Freestone trout rivers. These are the large and mature valley river systems that gather several mountain creeks or a smaller number of foothill streams. They tend to have the classic riffle/run/pool structure, but all written large. The habitat types preferred by different insect species are broader and, because of the size of the water, more isolated. As a consequence, hatches are more often than not concentrated into a single insect or at most two or sometimes three insects, rather than the constant arrival of a wide variety of species that keeps trout from feeding selectively. On big water, selectivity is more often the rule, less often the exception. You'll usually find insects emerging, and trout focused on them, in a single water type: now in riffles, then in runs, at times in pools, very often on big flats. If terrestrials are the main food source, trout will usually gather along the banks. Always choose your imitations based on the water type where you find trout feeding in big rivers.

Spring creeks arise from stable sources. They have bottoms composed of finer materials than freestone streams. Insects and crustaceans live in the myriads of microniches found in rooted vegetation beds. You'll be served by collecting and matching trout food forms on spring creeks more than on most other stream types.

Spring creeks. The term *spring creek* defines a stream or river's origins more than it does its water type. But springs are constant, and streams that originate in them have stable flows and are not subject to spates, and therefore tend to have silt, sand, or marl bottoms rather than the cobbled structure of freestone streams. They also allow vegetation to take root; it is not scoured out by rainstorms or spring snowmelt. Stable flows, silty bottoms, and vegetation beds all lend themselves to a set of insects that is often different from those found in freestone streams. Because spring creeks lack the wide variety of habitats found in less stable waters, their insect species, and crustaceans as well, tend to be more restricted. You won't find a wide variety, but you will find each insect or crustacean in much greater numbers.

Spring creek hatches tend to be concentrated, and trout tend to feed selectively on them. You're most likely to need to match a hatch on these waters. Because the surface tends to be smooth, your imitation often must be fairly exact. Your tackle should be light; your presentations delicate.

Tailwaters. A dam can be constructed on a stream of any size, in any type of terrain. The resulting tailwater will vary depending on how large the dam is and on the gradient downstream from it. But most Western tailwaters are formed by dams on medium to large rivers in the downstream reaches of mature river systems. The reservoir formed upstream naturally submerges whatever river system existed there. The most beneficial dams, in terms of trout fishing, are those built in the reaches of rivers that were previously warmwater fisheries. The depths of a reservoir cool the water; the release downstream becomes suitable to trout for a few to many miles, until the water once again warms up and will no longer support them.

Food types downstream from dams, similar to those on spring creeks, tend to be restricted in variety but great in abundance. As a consequence, you often find it necessary to match the food forms that cause selective feeding, which could be scuds or aquatic worms as often as midges or mayflies.

Tailwaters take many shapes and have a few different flow regimens. Some have reregulating dams that stabilize flows after power is generated. These are the most stable and also safest to fish. Others are used for irrigation and are best fished in fall, winter, and early spring, when water is being stored and flows downstream are low. A few Western tailwaters are used for power generation and have no rereg dams. These are subject to sudden increases in flow and can be dangerous if you aren't aware that they're suddenly rising. They are also the least stable for insect populations, often best fished with nymphs that imitate aquatic worms or sow bugs.

3 Hatch Timing in the West

Anglers always want nature to fit into consistent patterns. I'd like to be able to report that the Western Green Drake hatch will begin to show up everywhere in the West on the first day of June, year after year, that it will reach its peak and incite trout to riot between the fourth and fourteenth, that it will then taper off for a week, and trout will turn their interest toward Pale Morning Duns, which begin to emerge on the fifteenth of June. But insect hatches are far from this predictable, even on a single trout stream. Hatch timing is dependent on many things: weather, stream flows, snowpack, and some things that biologists haven't figured out yet.

Photoperiod, or the amount of daily daylight, is about the only key to insect hatches that is a constant. It lengthens day by day each spring and contracts at the same rate each autumn, year on year forever into the future, we hope. Aquatic insects mature as nymphs, or enter pupation from the larval stage, timed to the annual light cycle: a year-class of a specific insect species will be ready for its transition to the next stage in life during an appropriate window of time that is consistent. Emergence within that window will depend on factors that are more variable.

Water temperature is a key factor. We know that many insects, such as the great Salmonflies, begin to emerge when water temperatures approach a magic 50 degrees F. Not all insects obey this trigger, but the hatches of those that do will often move upstream predictably, following rising water temperatures toward the headwaters. Water temperature is affected by the average daily temperature of the atmosphere. The amount of snowpack also affects water temperature. Water will remain colder later in high snowpack years and warm up earlier if snow is out of the system sooner. These are reasons rising global temperatures advance hatches, some of which now begin an average of a few days to a week or more earlier than they did fifty years ago.

Water levels might trigger hatches, though this is not certain. It is clear that some hatches aren't affected by high water. The Salmonfly hatch on the lower Yellowstone River usually happens when the river is still too blown out with snowmelt to fish. The Mother's Day Caddis hatch on the same river happens in some years before runoff and provides excellent fishing. In other years the same hatch happens during high and muddy flows and fishing is a bust. Clearly, our ability to fish with pleasure and hope of success is affected by both water levels and clarity.

Daily weather conditions cause hatches to intensify or to hold off. If the weather turns bitter, insects seem to know it and will wait it out. If the wind is fierce, insects will often wait to hatch. I just spent three days on a pond during the Speckle-Wing (*Callibaetis*) hatch. Normally, I'd have had three hours of dry-fly fishing each day over big noses poking out to sip duns. The wind never relented, however, and I had a total of just half an hour fishing over trout rising to a few windblown duns.

Prime conditions for emergence, especially of mayflies, are usually light rain or at least a cloud cover. This prevents dehydration, a major danger to most aquatic insects. Hatches on rainy and even snowy days are often longer and heavier than they are on bright days. I've seen the Western March Brown hatch go on for several hours on gloomy days and then abruptly stop on a sunny day, only to begin again when the weather again began to snort. The heaviest March Brown hatch I've ever fished was in a violent April rainstorm on Oregon's Deschutes River.

Because the West is so large, two factors have to be taken into account when predicting hatch timing. The first is the progression from south to north. The weather naturally warms first in southern latitudes, and later in the north. A species of insect that hatches over the broad range of the entire West will begin earlier in southern California, Arizona, and New Mexico than it will in Idaho and Montana. The difference can be several weeks.

Overlaid on the progression from south to north is altitude: the higher in the mountains you go, the colder the weather gets, and the later hatches will begin. An emergence of a single species might start a month later in a stream at five thousand feet than it does in one at a thousand feet, even if the two elevations are adjacent. The geological map of the West is essentially a ring of mountains—the High Sierra and Cascades on the west and the Rockies on the east, surrounding the Great Basin. This complicates any emergence table. A hatch might begin three weeks later in the mountains of California than it does at much lower altitudes in Idaho.

Western hatches will, as an oversimplified rule, begin earliest along the coast and in the southwest, and progress generally north and east, ending—emerging latest—in the high northern Rockies. I've fished the March Brown hatch in February in coastal Oregon, in May in the Great Basin of Idaho, and in July on the Yellowstone Plateau in Wyoming. The same hatch might always be in spring, but spring in southern California might be three months earlier than the same season in Yellowstone Park or the Canadian Rockies.

If you're a gardener, you can think of hatch progressions in the widely varied West as being fairly consistent with natural vegetation zones. Both blooms and hatches will begin earlier at warmer low elevations and southern latitudes, continue through modest altitudes and latitudes, and finish in the highest and most northern meadows.

Spring creeks, with their stabilized water temperatures, often confuse hatch timing of aquatic insects. Hatches that are consistently in spring on freestone streams might begin in midsummer

Spring Creeks are among the most beautiful places to fish in our great and varied West, but their hatches are not always in synch with those in freestone streams and tailwater rivers. You'll be far ahead on them if your fly boxes prepare you to fish whatever hatches might happen. If you fish a particular spring creek often, you'll be wise to begin at once to create your own hatch timing chart specifically for it.

on one spring creek and in fall on another. It's as if the constant water temperatures, the same no matter the season, have disconnected the insects' clocks.

This difficulty in precisely predicting dates for any emergence makes it a useful strategy to carry flies tied to match the major hatches at all times, so that you are prepared to fish them whenever, and wherever, you find them.

4 Tactics for Fishing Hatches

Because I've defined a *hatch* as any stage of any food form that causes selectivity, when matching the hatch you might have to present flies to feeding trout at any one of four levels: the surface, subsurface, mid-depths, and bottom. You'll need to rig differently to fish each level, and you'll also use different presentation methods at each of the levels to make your imitations act most like the real things upon which trout feed. Myriad minor ways have been devised to fish each level, but just a few essential rigs and methods form the basics. These will always be at the core of your fly fishing for trout. Learn the elemental rigs and methods, and know which one to use when you're faced with trout feeding on one stage of one food form and disdaining all else.

SURFACE

This is the level we always think about when we think about fishing hatches. It's where trout take most mayfly duns and spinners, caddis and stonefly adults, midges, ants, beetles and grasshoppers, and many other insects that arise from water or fall to it. It's the level at which you'll fish dry flies to imitate floating insects that ride the currents, or emergers that float flush to imitate insects trapped in the surface film, many of them struggling to break through it.

Your goal is generally to present a floating fly dead-drift, without drag from the leader. Drag, defined as any movement of your fly contrary to the way a current would move a natural insect, is almost always frightening to trout. It's caused most often by casting across conflicting tendrils of current. These draw your leader tight and scoot the fly unnaturally across the surface. You achieve the

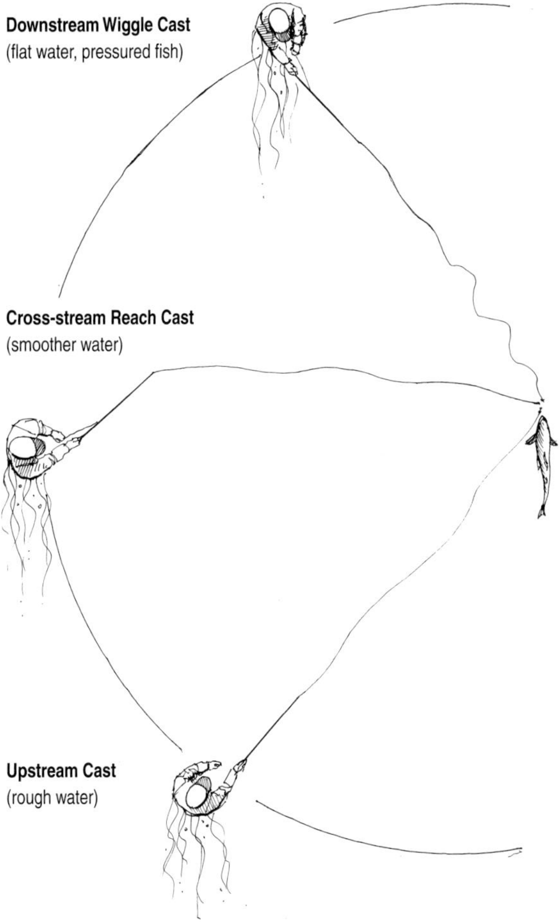
Downstream Wiggle Cast
(flat water, pressured fish)
Cross-stream Reach Cast
(smoother water)
Upstream Cast
(rough water)

desired dead-drift, drag-free float differently on different types of water, with upstream, cross-stream, and downstream presentations.

It's best to think of a rising trout as being at the center of a circle, facing upstream. Your casting positions are on the periphery of the circle around the trout. The best position will vary with the type of water in which the trout holds.

Upstream Dry-Fly Presentation

If a trout feeds in a riffle or choppy run, a downstream position and upstream cast will usually be your best choice. The broken surface prevents trout from noticing your line and fly going over its head in the air. The rough surface makes the leader much less noticeable on the water. Take your casting position as near to the trout as you can without alarming it. This reduces the number of conflicting currents between you and the trout, and reduces the chance of drag. Rather than standing directly downstream from the trout, position yourself at a slight angle to one side or the other. Your line and leader will alight on the water a bit to the side of the trout and float downstream at an angle off to its side. The trout will be less likely to be disturbed by your cast and drift.

Cross-Stream Reach Cast

On smoother runs and flats, if you cast upstream over the head of a rising trout, it will see your line in the air and probably think it's a kingfisher or osprey on the attack. If, during the float, the leader is visible up to the fly, a trout rising in smooth water is likely to notice it and refuse to take the fly. You must contrive a way to keep the line out of the trout's sight, and drift the fly downstream to the trout ahead of the leader, as if it's not attached to anything.

The cross-stream reach cast is a wonderful way to get a drag-free drift without alarming trout. Take your position off to the side of the rising trout, and get as near to it as you can without spooking it; again to get conflicting currents behind you. Measure your cast, aiming to place the fly from two to five feet upstream from the trout, and carry a few feet of extra line in the air. Direct your delivery stroke at the point where you want the fly to land. As the cast unfolds toward its target, lay your rod over in the upstream direction, and reach with your arm as far as you can. The fly will land where you want it, with the leader and then line stretching away from it, at an angle upstream to the rod tip.

As the fly drifts freely downstream toward the trout, follow it with your rod. This will keep the fly floating without drag. You can extend the drift by continuing to follow with your rod downstream, extending your arm in that direction. You always want to place the fly just upstream from a single rising trout that you've singled out. But the extended drift of a reach cast can let you fish a dead-drift presentation through a pod of several trout if the targeted trout refuses your fly or simply doesn't notice it.

Downstream Wiggle Cast

On the smoothest water, over trout that have been pestered by many other anglers, it's often necessary to present your dry fly or surface-film emerger without any hint that it might be attached to anything at all. The best way to achieve that is with the downstream wiggle cast. Once you've mastered the art of inserting slack into your line and leader by wobbling your rod tip back and forth as the line loop unfurls, you'll be able to use the same movement with the reach cast and make that tactic even more effective.

Your position for the wiggle cast should be upstream from a rising trout, but off to one side at a substantial angle. If you cast directly downstream, you'll get one good presentation; if the trout refuses, your leader and line will follow the fly over the trout's head. Your pickup for the next cast will lift everything off the water right in its sight. The trout will be spooked.

Aim your cast, as with all other dry-fly presentations, two to five feet upstream from a single rising trout. Time its rise rhythm, if you can, so it's about ready to take a natural when your fly arrives in front of it. Make your measuring casts well away from the trout, and carry a few feet of extra line in the air. Aim your delivery stroke directly at the point where you'd like your fly to land. As the line loop unfurls, wiggle the tip of your rod vigorously back and forth. The line and leader will land on the water in a series of S curves. It won't happen perfectly the first, or even the tenth, time you try it. It's a presentation that requires practice, some on the lawn or casting pond, but most on water where trout rise. A slight warning here: a rod that is too stiff will refuse to wiggle at all; one too soft will sweep back and forth so slowly that you can't get those nice curves drawn on the surface.

The fly should land in the trout's feeding lane at about the time the trout is poised to rise again. As the fly floats downstream toward the trout, the S curves in the line and leader straighten, allowing the imitation a drag-free drift. If the trout fails to come up for the fly on the first cast, don't worry; that is average. After the fly has gone past the trout a few feet, lay your rod over to the side. The line and leader will straighten and draw the fly away, out of the trout's sight.

If you make the wiggle cast delicately and accurately, you can repeat the presentation over and over to the same trout without putting it down. Such repeated drifts are often necessary to place the fly precisely in the trout's feeding lane, at exactly the moment it's ready to rise. Never set the hook abruptly when a trout takes your fly. Count a beat or two, or you'll snatch the fly right out of the trout's mouth.

SUBSURFACE

Many trout appear to take floating insects from the surface, but they're actually feeding on subsurface emergers or on nymphs and pupae approaching the surface for emergence. Trout also feed just beneath the surface on drowned mayfly duns and spinners, female caddis adults swimming down to lay their eggs on the bottom, small stoneflies trapped in currents after depositing their eggs, and even terrestrial insects that have fallen to the water and sunk an inch or two. The surest sign of subsurface feeding is a riseform that appears to be on top but leaves no bubbles afloat in the rise ring. The trout did not break the surface. You can fish all day over it with dry flies, and it will patiently ignore them. Always observe rises carefully. Learn to determine the trout's level, and which stage of what insect is being taken selectively.

The subsurface level is just one to six or so inches deep. Rigging and presentations for fishing subsurface are most often the same as those for fishing the surface. Just tie a sunk fly to your tippet instead of a dry: a subsurface emerger, winged or wingless wet fly, soft-hackled wet, an unweighted nymph, or even a small beadhead or lightly weighted nymph. Successfully using a size 16 or 18 Pheasant Tail Nymph during a Blue-Winged Olive hatch is a perfect example of fishing subsurface when trout appear to be taking duns on top, but often are not.

Strike Indicator and Subsurface Imitation

Sometimes it's wise to add a small indicator three to five feet up the leader from a subsurface fly. That helps you follow the drift of the invisible fly and makes it far easier to notice takes. When fishing a subsurface fly with an indicator to visible rising trout, use the same set of presentations you would with a floating fly: upstream, cross-stream, or downstream wiggle cast.

Dry Fly and Dropper

Another way to fish a subsurface fly inches deep is to rig it as a dropper from a dry fly. The basic rules for a dry and dropper rig call for a floating fly one or two sizes larger than the sunk fly, so the dry will not be pulled under, and a tippet to the sunk fly that is one size finer than the tippet to the dry, so that when you lose the subsurface fly, you don't lose everything. The tippet for the dropper should be tied to the hook bend of the dry with an improved clinch knot. It should be eighteen inches to about three feet long. Use the same set of upstream, cross-stream, and downstream presentations already outlined.

Hidy Subsurface Swing

Pete Hidy was co-author with James Leisenring of *The Art of Tying the Wet Fly & Fishing the Flymph*. Hidy's term *flymph* refers to an insect that is no longer a nymph, but not yet a perfect fly, hence a flymph. Today we call them emergers. Flymphs are tied to fish just a few inches deep. To apply the Hidy subsurface swing, tie a flymph to your standard dry-fly leader tippet, and position yourself at a 30- to 60-degree angle upstream and across from a rising trout or small pod of them. Place your flymph on the water about a foot upstream from the trout and two to four feet beyond it. Immediately give the fly a slight tug to submerge it. Then keep the rod low and the line

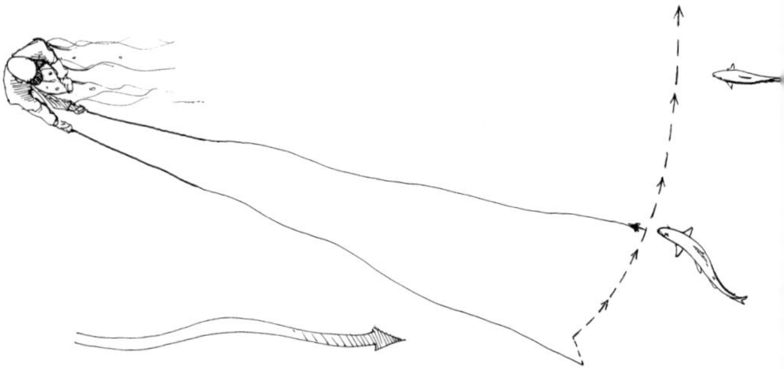

The Hidy subsurface swing is effective in situations where trout feed so near the surface that they send rise rings to the top, but there are no bubbles in those rings, so they're obviously taking something just under the surface. If any adult insects are on the water or in the air, match them with a flymph or wet fly. Trout are probably taking them submerged. Take your position upstream and across from the working trout, cast slightly upstream and beyond them, pop the fly under, and then let it swing in front of the trout. They'll usually intercept it as it swims past.

tight to coax the fly into a swing right in front of the feeding fish, or through the pod. Follow the swing with the rod tip. It's always wise to single out a trout, but it's also smart to show your fly on the rest of the swing to several others if they're feeding nearby and the first trout refuses.

MID-DEPTHS

When nymphs or pupae leave the bottom for emergence, or when adults swim to the bottom to lay their eggs, they must pass through the mid-depths. Trout sometimes take stations mid-water and feed on naturals passing in front of them. At such times you'll want to fish a foot or two down. Though the mid-depths are often considered the realm of wet flies, you can fish nymphs effectively in the same zone. Streamers can also entice trout when fished a foot or two deep, especially when the water is just three to four feet deep.

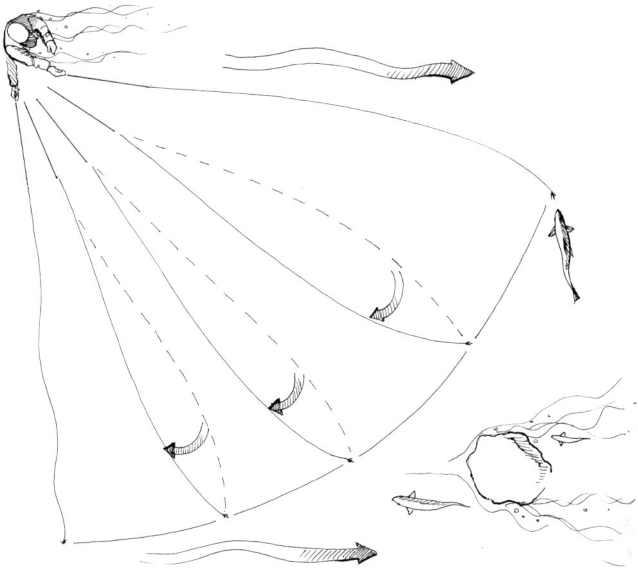

The standard wet fly, nymph, and streamer swing is highly effective against trout stationed and feeding in the mid-depths. Make your cast across the current, higher into it if the water is fast, lower down if it is slow. Mend constantly while your fly sinks, and then come tight against it and tease it into its swing.

Wet Fly, Nymph, or Streamer Swing

In most trout water, you can do most of your mid-depth fishing with floating lines. The leader should be a foot or two longer than the rod and tapered to a tippet that is in balance with the size fly you'll be casting. If the current is swift, or the water deep enough that the mid-depths are a bit farther down, you might find it necessary to use a wet-tip or clear intermediate line with a slightly shorter leader.

Your position for the swing should be upstream and across from the trout you're covering, at a distance that is a comfortable cast for you, not a stretch. Make your initial cast across stream, at an angle either slightly downstream, straight across, or slightly upstream. The speed of the current, and the depth you desire your fly to obtain, will determine the exact angle of your cast. The faster the current, and the more depth you want, the higher upstream you make your cast.

As soon as the fly lands on the water, make at least one big mend, and follow with several more mends as the fly sinks and moves downstream. When it has reached the position of the trout, and at the same time the depth you deem correct, then let the line draw tight against the rod tip and coax the fly into a slow swing. Cover the fish thoroughly with subsequent casts, and explore the water downstream by taking a short step after fishing out each swing. If a trout plucks at the fly, don't yank. Let it set the hook itself.

Indicator and Weighted Nymph

This is essentially the same rig, and the same tactic, that is employed with a floating line and strike indicator for subsurface flies. Use a longer three- to five-foot tippet between the indicator and the nymph, or even pair of them. It's the perfect mid-depth rig for weighted nymphs, or nymphs tied with tungsten beads.

Your position should be downstream from the trout holding and feeding in the mid-depths, and off to one side so you don't line them. Make your casts five to fifteen feet upstream from the trout. Follow the drift of your indicator with your rod tip. Avoid letting your line tug at the indicator, because that lifts the nymph, and it will pass over the heads of the trout. Repeat the cast as often as necessary to make sure trout have a chance to notice the nymph, or pair of them. If you find trout feeding in the mid-depths in one type of water, after you've fished that water out, move upstream or down to find the same type of water, and fish it whether you see trout there or not. It's likely they'll be doing the same thing in similar situations.

BOTTOM

Most of your fishing along the bottom will be searching fishing to trout feeding opportunistically rather than selectively and therefore

Rigging with an indicator and weighted nymph, or brace of them, will let you fish dead-drift presentations to trout suspended in the mid-depths. Make your casts upstream, and tend each drift to keep the fly, or flies, at the depth you want, tumbling along freely. You don't want drag any more here than you would if you were fishing a dry fly, though it's not likely to be as fatal.

not in the province of a book about hatches. However, when a single food form becomes both abundant and available along the bottom, trout will feed as selectively there as they do on top. The same rigging and tactics apply to both searching and imitative situations.

When trout feed selectively along the bottom, you'll need to collect with a net, or make a guess at what they're taking down there. At times they'll be feeding on large insects such as Salmonfly nymphs. Most times they'll be focused on smaller mayfly nymphs, caddis larvae, or crustaceans such as aquatic sow bugs.

Strike Indicator and Split Shot Nymphing

Unless you know precisely what trout are taking, it's usually sound strategy to rig with a size 12 to 16 beadhead nymph, and a small size 16 to 20 trailer nymph such as a Pheasant Tail Flashback. Fix a strike

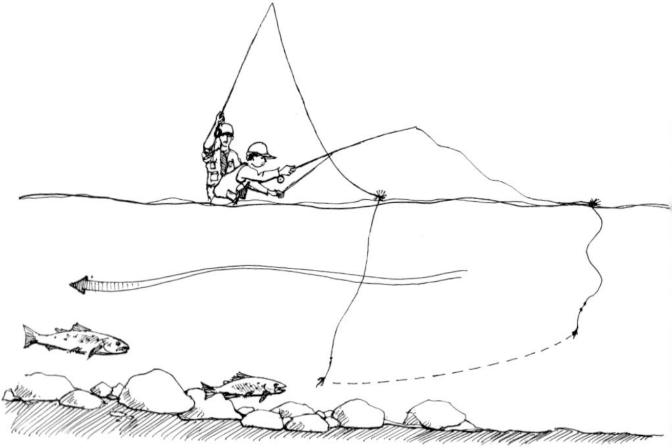

The indicator-and-shot rig is the gold standard for nymphing, whether you're fishing over selective trout, as we are in this book, or simply searching the water, exploring for trout, using your nymphs as your eyes to find fish. The concept is the same: get your nymph, or pair of them, right to the bottom, and keep them tumbling along there without drag, if you can.

indicator on the leader one-and-a-half to two times the water depth above the point fly. Add one or two split shot to the leader at the tippet knot. Tie your nymphs eight to twelve inches apart. The amount of weight on the leader, and the length of leader to the indicator, depend on the water depth and current speed. Be prepared to adjust your rig to get your flies to the depth of feeding trout.

Take your position downstream and to one side of the trout. Place your casts ten to fifteen feet upstream from them. Make an immediate roll-mend to toss your indicator upstream from the nymphs without lifting the nymphs out of the water. This allows them to sink much faster and to drift without drag from the indicator. Mend frequently to keep your indicator from leading, and therefore pulling, the nymphs downstream. The dead drift of the indicator is your best indication that those nymphs are tumbling freely with the current, as they should. Unless you've pinpointed the lie of a particular trout, cover all of the bottom within reach, with short casts, before changing positions to cover a new bit of bottom.

When indicator-and-shot nymphing, be prepared to constantly change your casting position, the amount of weight on your leader, and the length of leader between your indicator and flies. It's generally more effective to change your rigging than it is to change flies when you're not catching trout along the bottom. The single change in all of fly fishing that I have found to improve my luck most often, and most abruptly, is the addition of another split shot to an indicator-and-shot rig.

STILLWATERS

Trout feed on a narrower range of food forms in stillwaters than they do in streams. Your fly selection will provide far more trout for you if it reflects those food forms. I always recommend carrying a separate large fly box that is dedicated strictly to your favorite lake fly patterns.

All of the essential Western stillwater trout foods are covered in this book. Even during your explorations of lakes and ponds when nothing is hatching, you'll catch more trout by using imitations of food forms dominant in stillwaters, because those are the things trout are accustomed to seeing and eating. When trout do feed selectively, you'll have just the right flies.

Surface

When you spot rising trout, move into position to cover them without spooking them. Usually that will require a float tube, pontoon boat, pram, or boat, though sometimes you can reach rising trout by casting from shore or by wading. Stillwater trout often travel and feed in pods, rather than as singles. Always try to position yourself a modest cast away from the edge of a pod, rather than right in the middle of it, where you're more likely to put them down than catch them.

If trout in a pod rise consistently, it's always best to cast to those at the edge of the pod nearest you, rather than lining those to reach trout in the middle or on the far side. It's better to place your fly

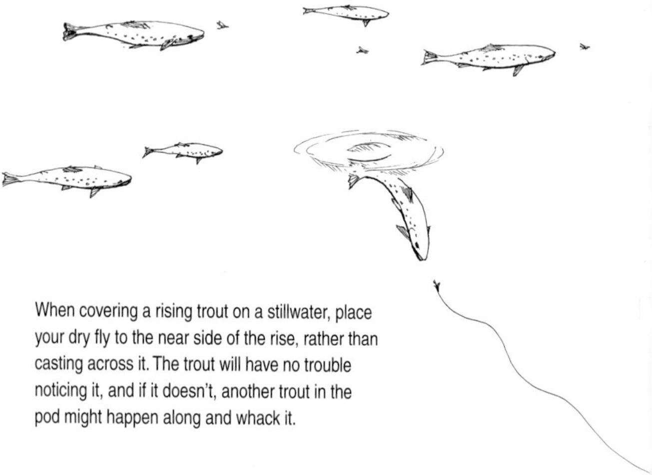

When covering a rising trout on a stillwater, place your dry fly to the near side of the rise, rather than casting across it. The trout will have no trouble noticing it, and if it doesn't, another trout in the pod might happen along and whack it.

near a recent rise, and let it sit there a reasonable time, than it is to constantly lift it and paste it into every next rise. A trout is likely to come along soon enough and notice your fly. If you tear the water up with constant casting, you're likely to put all of the trout down.

When you cover a specific rise with a dry fly, make your first cast a foot or two to your side of the rise. If the trout is still lingering near the surface, you won't line it. Let that cast marinate a minute or more; the trout will probably come back. If it doesn't, make your next cast about ten feet to one side or the other, preferably in the direction the trout was going when it rose, if you can ascertain that. Usually you can't and are forced to guess.

The most satisfying situation, when fishing rising trout on a stillwater, is to piece together a series of rises and calculate when and where the trout will come up next. Set your dry fly right there, ahead of time, and if the trout doesn't turn, or your fly is not completely wrong, a nose will come confidently out of the water and take your fly.

If you notice a trout rising in a straight line in a lake or pond and can figure out the most likely locus of its next rise, place your fly there. Set the hook slowly when that nose lofts out and falls slowly onto your dry, or you'll pull the fly right away from the trout.

There are two situations when you want to impart action to a stillwater dry fly. The first is during an evening rise to adult midges, which the British call *buzzers*. These scoot across the water, and trout take them on the move. Choose a hackled dressing. Cast it ahead of a rising trout. Skate it a few inches to attract the trout's attention, and then let it sit. The second is during a hatch of Traveling Sedges, usually in lakes in British Columbia or Alberta, though I've also seen caddis travel in many other Western stillwaters. Use a dressing designed to skate. When you see a rise—or as often hear it!—set your fly as near to it as you can and skitter it out of there. If the trout detonates on it and you set hard and snap your leader, don't blame me.

Shallow Sunk Wet Flies and Nymphs

In a few situations, trout take natural insects so near the surface that they appear to be taking floating adults. Examples are migrating damselfly nymphs, which travel near the surface, and alderfly adults, which are so dense that they sink at once. To fish nymph or wet-fly imitations shallow, rig with the same floating line you use for dry flies, or switch to a clear intermediate sinking line.

If you see damsel nymphs, tie on an appropriate nymph imitation. If it's alders, or perhaps flying ants, use the ancient Alder or a Black Gnat wet fly. With either nymphs or wets, cast to cover rises, let the fly sink, and then begin a slow retrieve. If rises are scattered, cast out in the area where they're occurring, again let the fly sink, and begin a patient retrieve. Sometimes a stripping retrieve will animate the fly and attract trout. Most often, though, the slowest retrieve produces the fastest fishing.

Visible Plant Beds, Shallows, and Shoals

Sometimes you can look down into clear water and see the bottom, or plant beds, and even more rarely, see trout cruising over the bottom, or around and through those beds. When you do, you know exactly the depth you need to fish and can select a line with a sink rate that will get your fly down to the trout. You'll have to guess which fly will work, but plant beds have lots of damsel nymphs, scuds, and a few other things, all of which will be olive for camouflage. Select an imitative pattern in that color, size 12 or 14, and it's likely trout will be happy to take it.

Anchor within a moderate cast of the bed. Make your casts over the bed, and then patiently count your fly down. A good rule is to count for fifteen seconds on the first cast, twenty on the the second, twenty-five on the third, and so on until you catch weeds, snags, or trout. Calculate subsequent casts accordingly. If it's weeds or snags, shorten up the count. If it's trout, repeat what worked.

Indicator Fishing in Stillwaters

Midge pupae are among the most important trout food forms in almost all lakes and ponds. They make themselves available to trout in two primary ways: either staged and hanging one to two feet above the bottom, waiting for their ascent to the surface, or staged and hanging just a few inches beneath the surface, waiting for the right moment to emerge through it. The best way to imitate them is to suspend one or two pupa patterns beneath a strike indicator, either just above the bottom or just under the surface.

For average depths, from a foot for subsurface trout to water about ten or twelve feet deep, use a yarn indicator, leader tippet of a

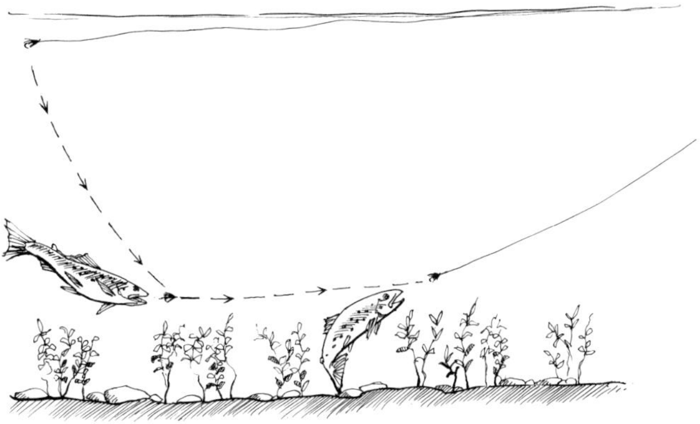

If you can see plant beds down below and, even better, can spot trout working them, then anchor and choose a line with a sink rate that will reach the depth at which you've noticed things happening. Cast out, count your fly down, and then bring it back with the slowest hand-twist retrieve you can manage. The slow retrieve not only mimics the movement of many natural insects, it also keeps your fly in the strike zone for the longest possible time.

single diameter, and a split shot or pinch of putty weight to get your fly or flies down, if needed. For deeper water, find the right depth by clipping your hemostat to the end of your leader tippet, again of a single diameter, and dropping it to the bottom. Lift your hemostat about eighteen inches from the bottom, reach over and grasp your leader where it enters the water, cut it, and tie in a blood knot at that point. Use a sliding hard indicator and shot or putty for a faster sink. When the pupae arrive at the proper depth, and the indicator seats itself against the knot in your leader, your flies will be suspended just off the bottom. You can fish fifteen to thirty feet deep with this rig. Pay close attention to the indicator. If it twitches, things are about to be over down there. If you don't set the hook quickly, the trout will be long gone.

PART TWO

Western Creek, Stream, and River Hatches

5 Mayflies

Mayflies are often referred to as the perfect fly rod insect. First, they require clean, cold water, which coincides with the needs of trout, so mayflies are almost always found in waters inhabited by trout. Second, most mayflies, though not all, emerge in open water, on the surfaces of streams and rivers, and stillwaters as well, adrift or riding the currents, where trout can get at them, and where we can cast our imitations of them. Third, the chosen mayfly survival tactic is mass emergence. They come off in such great numbers, in such a condensed span of time, that trout and birds simply can't eat them all. Fourth, most mayflies hatch during the light of day, when we can see it all happening and put into movement our own predatory calculations against the trout that feed on them. Last in the list of mayfly perfections is their beauty: the grace of form and movement and those gorgeous colors, all of which we try to imitate with our flies.

LIFE CYCLE

Mayflies have incomplete metamorphosis. They lack the pupal stage enjoyed by the butterfly or the caddisfly. The individual mayfly lives in the water as a nymph for all but a few days of its life cycle. All growth takes place in this stage, which usually lasts a year, but in some cases lasts only a few weeks, and in others lasts two years. What we anglers refer to as the *emerger* stage is the brief transition between the nymph and winged dun stages. The nymphal skin splits along the back, and the dun escapes. This can happen on the bottom, in the mid-depths, just subsurface, in the surface film itself, or on protruding rocks or grasses alongside the stream.

Mayflies live along the bottom, or on rooted vegetation, in the nymph stage, for most of their usual one-year life cycle.

The dun stage is what we think about when we think of imitating mayflies. This beautiful winged stage sometimes rides the surface for ten to twenty or more feet before its wings are dry and it is ready for flight. Trout applaud that, and so do we.

Mayfly spinners mate in the air, and then the females return to the water to deposit their eggs before falling to the surface spent, where they die or are eaten by trout.

The mayfly dun rides the surface until its wings are dry and hardened for flight. Then it flies to streamside vegetation. In half an hour to a couple of days, the dun sheds another skin and turns into the mature spinner, ready to mate. Mating takes place in the air, another bit of incomparable grace. The female spinner deposits her eggs back to the water and then collapses spent.

Variations in the way a mayfly species emerges, rides the water, and returns to lay its eggs determine how important each of its stages are. A species that masses as nymphs, emerges in the surface film, rides the water a long way as duns, and then returns to fall spent on good trout water will be important in all of its stages. A mayfly species that emerges sporadically by crawling out on rocks and then deposits its eggs at night might be big and beautiful and abundant, but trout won't usually get a chance to feed selectively on any of its stages.

These factors came into play when selecting the stages of mayflies to highlight in this book. Recall that the key criteria for inclusion is selective feeding by trout. If a stage of a mayfly, whether nymph, dun, or spinner, does not meet that criteria, it's not included.

Nymph Variations

Mayfly nymphs are broken into four categories, based on their behavior. They're classed as *swimmers, crawlers, clingers,* or *burrowers*.

Swimmers are minnowlike in shape and behavior. They're slender and tapered and most have fringed tails, all for better swimming. They live along the bottom or in rooted vegetation and dart from place to place with brisk movements. When in the drift, the smaller forms, such as the Blue-Winged Olives (*Baetis*), rest and are therefore best imitated with dead-drift presentations. Larger forms, such as the Gray Drakes (*Siphlonurus*) swim swiftly and can best be imitated with retrieves suitable for streamers.

Crawlers are generally much blockier in shape and have stout legs with which they crawl among rocks on the bottom, sometimes in fast currents. They do not swim well, and when knocked into the current they either tumble freely or swim feebly until they are able to get back to the bottom or get eaten by a trout.

Mayfly swimmer nymphs are long, slender, and streamlined for swimming. Their gills are flat, platelike, and always along the sides of the abdominal segments. The tails are often fringed for more efficient swimming.

Mayfly crawler nymphs are typically blocky, with stout legs, and tails without thick fringes. They're poor swimmers, and your imitations should be fished to tumble freely near the bottom.

Mayfly clinger nymphs are flat as Frisbees. They cling so tightly to rocks that they are rarely available to trout except in migratory moments before emergence. They're not often included among the important stages of a mayfly species because they seldom cause selective feeding.

Clingers are designed by nature to live in the swiftest currents. Their bodies are flattened. Their eyes have migrated to the tops of their heads. Their legs are flat and strong. These mayfly nymphs are so thin that they're able to live in the millimeters-thick layer of water slowed by friction as the current races over rocks in riffles and even rapids.

Mayfly burrower nymphs are almost always large. They are very capable swimmers, dashing to the top to emerge into the dun stage. Trout sometimes key on this stage during hatches, which usually happen just at dark.

Burrowers are long, slender, and have fringed tails. Their gills are plumelike and wave in sequence over their backs to move fresh water through their burrows. Their front legs are short and shovel-shaped for digging. They either excavate a burrow in a mud or silt bottom, or they bury themselves in soft, sandy or pebbled bottoms. They're nearly all nocturnal, only coming out at night to feed on bottom detritus.

Blue-Winged Olive nymph

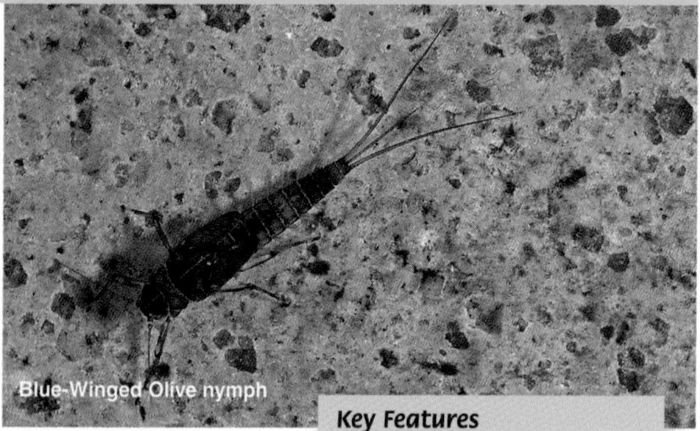
Blue-Winged Olive nymph

Common names: Blue-Winged Olive nymph, BWO nymph, Little Olive nymph

Latin name: *Baetis tricaudatus* (13 related Western species, 3 related genera: *Acentrella*, *Diphetor*, and *Plauditus)*

Size range: #16–22 (3–12 mm, ⅛–½ inch excluding tails)

Key Features

Tails: Two or three; if three, center tail usually shorter

Gills: Small, single, and oval on abdominal segments 1-7 or 2-7

Antennae: Two times or more longer than width of head

Body shape: Slender, tapered, and streamlined

Color: Olive to olive-brown to dark brown

Habitat

BWO nymphs are found in all kinds of creek, stream, and river habitats. They live in slow, moderate, or fast currents, in the clean gravel of freestone riffles or in gentle spring creeks and tailwaters. BWO nymphs thrive in aquatic plant beds. The likelihood of selective feeding increases as current speeds decrease. You're more likely to find trout feeding on them selectively in spring creeks and tailwaters than you are in freestone streams.

Emergence

BWOs normally go through two to three generations a year. Hatches can take place in every month. The first brood usually peaks in March, April, or May; the second in September or October. They emerge daily during the warmest part of the day, between 11 a.m. and 3 p.m., though in summer it might be in morning or evening. They emerge in the surface film. BWO nymphs are often taken selectively, even when duns are on the surface.

Behavior and Tactics

When trout feed selectively during a BWO hatch, it's critical to notice whether trout focus on nymphs. Watch a few duns as they float through rises. If you see no duns disappear, suspect that trout are taking more nymphs than duns. Suspend one of the listed nymph patterns beneath your dry imitation, or if that dry fly fails to support it, replace the dry with a small yarn indicator. Use at least three feet of 5X or 6X tippet. Fish the nymph to rises exactly as you would a dry, with a drag-free subsurface drift.

Known Hatches

Yakima R., WA; Deschutes R., OR; Henrys Fork and Silver Creek, ID; South Platte R., CO; Hat Creek and Hot Creek, CA; San Juan R., NM; Green R., UT; Yellowstone R., WY; Bighorn R., Missouri R., and Paradise Valley spring creeks, MT; Bow R., AB.

Blue-Winged Olive dun

Blue-Winged Olive dun

Common names: Blue-Winged Olive, BWO, Little Olive dun
Latin name: *Baetis tricaudatus* (13 related Western species, 3 related genera: *Acentrella*, *Diphetor*, and *Plauditus)*
Size range: #16–22 (3–10 mm, ⅛–⅜ inch excluding tails)

Key Features

Tails: Two
Body color: Olive to olive-brown to dark brown or gray
Forewings: Trailing edge with short, paired veinlets; pale gray to dark slate gray
Hindwings: Small, long, and narrow; sometimes absent
Eyes: Male eyes large and turbanlike

Habitat

BWO duns arise from all moving water types. Many nymphs living in fast water make some migratory movement out of the rough water before emergence. BWO duns in freestone streams are most likely to be important on flats, in eddies, and in gentler edge flows alongside fast riffles and runs. BWO duns hatch in the heaviest numbers and are most important on spring creek and tailwater flats.

Emergence

BWO duns begin emerging in January. Hatches peak in April and May, taper off in summer, then peak again in fall, and trickle off through December. Daily hatches are in the afternoon. BWO hatches are heaviest under clouds, in rain, or even in snow. During light rain the hatch can last for two or three hours; in sunshine only half an hour. BWO duns emerge in the surface film and often float several feet before flying, especially if the weather is cool.

Behavior and Tactics

Trout work BWO hatches greedily, often setting up positions high in the water column so they can sip duns constantly. If more than one mayfly species hatches at the same time—often a larger Pale Morning Dun, in what is called a *masking hatch*—trout prefer the BWO duns and ignore the bigger bites. If you're fishing freestone waters, you can often get away with ten-foot 5X leaders and upstream presentations. On smoother spring creek and tailwater currents, extend your tippet (usually 6X) to at least three feet. Fish with cross-stream reach or downstream wiggle casts.

Known Hatches

Though they are famous for their emergences on the waters listed in the nymph section, you should be prepared to fish BWO duns on any Western creek, stream, or river. The BWO is considered by many experts to be the most important single insect hatch.

Blue-Winged Olive spinner

Blue-Winged Olive spinner

Common names: BWO spinner; Blue Quill spinner, Red Quill spinner

Latin name: *Baetis tricaudatus* (13 related Western species, 3 related genera: *Acentrella*, *Diphetor*, and *Plauditus*)

Size range: #16–22 (3–10 mm, ⅛–⅜ inch excluding tails)

Key Features

Tails: Two

Body color: Male abdomen clear, reddish, or gray; female, light to dark reddish brown

Forewings: Trailing edge with short, paired veinlets; clear; glassy

Hindwings: Small, long, and narrow; sometimes absent

Eyes: Male eyes large, divided, and turbanlike

Habitat

Trout feed selectively on BWO spinners in freestone streams, but only on smooth water, usually flats or tailouts of pools. Trout feed selectively on spinnerfalls of BWOs most often on the flats of spring creeks and tailwaters. Because their mating flights usually form over the edges, rather than midstream, quiet eddies and side channels are the best places to look for trout sipping them.

Emergence

BWO spinnerfalls follow the seasonal patterns of duns, peaking in spring, tapering off in summer, and peaking again in fall. Daily peaks are in late afternoon to early evening. When trout sip in calm water, it can be difficult to see what they're taking. Use your aquarium net to seine the currents and your magnifying glass to examine the meshes. Often you'll find BWO spinners that are almost invisible to you, but not to the trout.

Behavior and Tactics

Many BWO spinners lay their eggs on the bottom, but selective feeding occurs most often to females that are spent, lying flat on the water on the smoothest surfaces. Refine your tackle, and use your most delicate tactics. This is the place for 2- to 4-weight lines, and fifteen-foot leaders tapered to long 6X and sometimes 7X tippets. The cross-stream reach and downstream wiggle casts will show your floating imitation to trout ahead of the line and leader, a necessity for this type of fishing.

Known Hatches

Refer to the list of known hatches under BWO nymphs. But don't restrict yourself to those rivers; wherever the water is smooth and BWO hatches heavy, you might need spinner imitations.

Brown Dun

Brown dun

Common names: Brown Dun, Gray Drake dun, *Ameletus* dun
Latin name: *Ameletus* (26 Western species)
Size range: #10–12 (10–14 mm, ½–⅝ inch excluding tails)

Key Features

Tails: Two
Body color: Brown, yellow-brown, or olive, some with distinct black markings
Forewings: Mottled brown to olive-brown
Hindwings: Large, with sharp projection on leading edge
Eyes: Males eyes large, meet on top of head

Habitat

Ameletus are distributed in almost all moving water types, from swift headwater streams to smooth spring creeks. They're most abundant along quiet grassy or rocky edges or beneath undercut banks. I've never seen nymphs or spinners taken selectively. Duns do not emerge in open water but can be blown in along the edges. They're referred to as Gray Drakes on some Montana streams, though Brown Dun is usually a more accurate description.

Emergence

Ameletus can hatch at almost any time of year, but they're most important in late spring and early fall. The nymphs crawl out on protruding vegetation or rocks before the duns emerge. Duns will be available to trout only near the banks, most often in very smooth water, and almost always when the wind huffs sufficiently to drive at least a few to the water. They are large, and trout will move into the shallows to feed on them.

Brown Compara-dun

Behavior and Tactics

Brown Duns, or Gray Drakes as they're as often called, can often be spotted on rocks at the rocky edges of riffles and runs on freestone streams or on grass stems protruding from spring creeks. If the wind is high enough, a few will be blown onto nearby peaceful edge flows. This combination of an emergence with windy weather is most common in spring. Watch for scattered but bold rises near shore. Cover them with upstream-and-across casts unless the trout prove so finicky that you're forced to move into position for reach casts or wiggle casts.

Known Hatches

Skagit R., BC; Fall R., OR; Bitterroot R., MT. I've collected representative Brown Dun nymphs from nearly every small, medium, and large stream I've sampled, in every state and province in the West.

Gray Drake nymph

Common names: Gray Drake nymph, Black Drake nymph
Latin name: *Siphlonurus occidentalis* (4 related Western species)
Size range: #10–12 (10–20 mm, 3/8–3/4 inch excluding tails)

Key Features

Tails: Three, equal in length, fringed with hairs
Gills: Large, platelike, double on segments 1-2 or 1-7
Antennae: Short, less than two times width of head
Body shape: Tapered, streamlined
Body color: Light to dark gray, with darker markings on abdomen

Habitat

Gray Drake nymphs are strong swimmers but prefer the edges of quiet streams. They can be found in meadow reaches of freestone streams but are most abundant in spring creeks. Related species are common around the vegetated perimeters of lakes, where trout feed on them in shallows. When ready for emergence in moving water, these nymphs gather in great numbers in quiet backwaters, sometimes in areas too shallow for trout to reach them.

Emergence

Gray Drake nymphs are available to trout in scattered numbers through early and late spring. Then they begin to mass along the edges for early summer emergence periods. They gather in many Pacific coastal waters in late May and June, and in Rocky Mountain areas in late July and August. The nymphs crawl out of the water, usually on protruding grass and reed stems, before the dun escapes. Trout follow the nymphs into shallow water and take them whenever an opportunity presents itself.

Near Enough

Behavior and Tactics

The Gray Drake nymph is an agile swimmer. It spends most of its time at rest in aquatic vegetation at the edge of the stream or in quiet backeddies where plants have taken root. Polly Rosborough, author of *Tying and Fishing the Fuzzy Nymphs*, recommended rigging his Near Enough imitation on a wet-tip line, casting it out into the current, letting it swing to the edge, and then retrieving it like a streamer. You can also rig it on a floating line, cast it upstream along the edges, fish along undercuts, and retrieve it downstream just like a streamer.

Known Hatches

Williamson R. and Davis Lk., OR; Silver Ck. and lower Henrys Fork Snake, ID; Yellowstone R. in the park, WY. Populations are scattered throughout the West and can be found wherever the water is suitably slow and has grassy edges.

Gray Drake spinner

Gray Drake spinner

Common names: Gray Drake spinner, Black Drake spinner
Latin name: *Siphlonurus occidentalis* (4 related Western species)
Size range: #10–12 (10–20 mm, 3/8–3/4 inch excluding tails)

Key Features

Tails: Two
Body color: Wine-red to almost black, with distinct banding
Forewings: Clear, glassy
Hindwings: Large, with rounded leading edge
Eyes: Male eyes large, meet on top of head, with pale band

Habitat

Gray Drake spinners return to lay their eggs near the same quiet habitat where they, as nymphs, migrated to shore to emerge. Egg-laying typically takes place on smooth flows characteristic of spring creeks and meadow-stream reaches of freestone streams. I've also seen them lay their eggs in chattery little riffles in freestone streams with low gradients. They're a fairly common inhabitant of streams that are drawn down for irrigation.

Emergence

Gray Drake nymphs crawl out to emerge; the duns have little importance to anglers. Annual emergence and consequent spinnerfalls are usually in June and July in lowland regions, and in August and September in the Rockies. Spinner flights form in midmorning to midafternoon. These are large insects, and their spinnerfalls can be so intense that spent bodies mass on the surface in current lines and seams. Trout feed on them greedily when they do.

Black Drake Spinner

Behavior and Tactics

Gray Drake spinners often fall with semi-spent wings and struggle until their wings collapse. Watch for rising trout on smooth water, and present your fly with careful cross-stream or downstream casts. I once watched Polly Rosborough fish his Black Drake Spinner over a rising trout on his home Williamson River. He smacked the fly to the water upstream from the fish so hard that the fly sank and let it drift downstream to the trout, which he caught.

Known Hatches

See nymphs section for specific known hatches. The Gray Drake is widespread in Western waters, though found only where water types are suitable for it. Wherever you collect the nymphs, you'll find significant spinnerfalls and should be prepared to fish them.

Pale Morning Dun nymph

Common names: Pale Morning Dun nymph, PMD nymph

Latin name: *Ephemerella excrucians* (was *E. inermis*; 6 related species and 1 related genus, *Serratella*)

Size range: #14–18 (6–9 mm, ¼–½ inch excluding tails)

Key Features

Tails: Three, same length, with dense fringe of fine hairs

Gills: Small, oval, on abdominal segments 3-7

Body shape: Somewhat blocky, modest taper

Body color: Reddish brown to dark brown, often with olive cast

Legs: Distinctly banded

Habitat

These crawler nymphs are common in freestone, spring creek, and tailwater habitats. They prefer low-gradient riffles, runs, flats, and tailouts. Heaviest population densities are found in spring creek and tailwater flows that are stable and have at least modest growth of rooted vegetation. PMD nymphs are more important on larger streams and rivers than in smaller creeks and headwater streams.

Emergence

PMD nymphs are most important as victims of selective feeding, and models for imitation, in spring and early summer, just before and during emergence. The nymphs leave the bottom and swim feebly to the surface, where the dun struggles free of the nymphal shuck in the surface film. Many trout focus on nymphs, even when duns are available. This might begin as early as 9 a.m. and last for several hours. PMD emergences occur most often in early afternoon.

Behavior and Tactics

PMD nymphs live either along the bottom or in vegetation beds, in moderate currents. They are poor swimmers; when trout get a chance at one, it's usually tumbling helplessly. Rig with the standard indicator-and-shot method, and fish your PMD nymph on or near the bottom, usually as part of a two-fly rig. When a hatch is in progress, and you see PMD duns on the surface but few going down in rises, fish a PMD nymph shallow and dead-drift, rigged with a yarn indicator, or as part of a dry-and-dropper rig.

Known Hatches

Hat Creek, CA; Deschutes R., OR; Yakima R., WA; Frying Pan R., CO; Green R., WY; Bighorn R., MT; Bow R., AB. This short list of famous rivers can be misleading; PMDs can be found in almost every Western trout stream and are an important hatch in most of them.

Pale Morning Dun

Pale Morning Dun

Common names: Pale Morning Dun, PMD

Latin name: *Ephemerella excrucians* (was *E. inermis*; 6 related species and 1 related genus, *Serratella*)

Size range: #14–18 (6–9 mm, ¼–½ inch excluding tails)

Key Features

Tails: Three

Body color: Female, pale to bright yellow; male, reddish brown

Forewings: Female, yellowish gray to yellow; male, pale gray

Hindwings: Small, with distinct rounded leading edge

Eyes: Female eyes pale, often with black spot; male eyes large, reddish brown

Habitat

PMD hatches are most common on either flat water or mildly riffled reaches of stream. They are more common on streams and rivers of moderate to large size than they are on smaller waters. Their most famous hatches are on large and mature rivers, many of them tailwaters, but they happen on many freestone streams and rivers as well. Experts consider them the second most important Western hatch, just behind BWOs.

Emergence

PMD hatches begin in late May, continue through summer, and end in early September. Daily hatches begin as early as 9 a.m., but most are in late morning or early afternoon. The hatch can go on for hours on overcast days but can be much shorter when the sun shines. Duns emerge in the surface film or just beneath it. PMDs have a difficult time extracting their wings from the nymphal shuck; the species suffers an inordinate number of cripples.

Behavior and Tactics

PMD duns have more trouble getting off the water than many other mayfly species. They are often stuck in their shucks, as cripples, and just as often drift for long distances while their wings dry. They often flutter, attempting to lift off, but fail, falling back to the water. Because they often emerge on fairly smooth water, you should usually fish their imitations on long, fine leaders with reach casts or wiggle casts. However, if you aren't having luck enticing trout, try skating your fly just inches and then let it sit. That movement might make all the difference.

Known Hatches

Most famous Western streams and rivers have the PMD hatch. So do most Western waters that are not famous. Imitations of PMDs should be standard in your fly boxes; don't add them only when you'll be fishing waters where you know they'll be important.

Pale Morning Dun spinner

Pale Morning Dun spinner

Common names: Pale Morning Dun spinner, PMD spinner
Latin name: *Ephemerella excrucians* (was *E. inermis*; 6 related species and 1 related genus, *Serratella*)
Size range: #14–18 (6–9 mm, ¼–½ inch excluding tails)

Key Features

Tails: Three
Body color: Females, pale yellow-olive to tan; males, reddish brown
Forewings: Clear, glassy
Hindwings: Small, with distinct, rounded leading edge
Eyes: Females, pale, often with black spot; males, reddish brown

Habitat

PMD spinnerfalls are important only on waters where hatches of duns are fairly heavy. If hatches are somewhat sparse, the resulting spinnerfall will rarely be fishable. Flights of PMD males form over riffles and glides, and the spent females fall to the same water types. As with the nymphs and duns, they're most important in medium and large river systems, and least important in small and vigorous headwater streams.

Emergence

PMD female spinners return to the water to drop their eggs or to wash the egg clusters off by dipping their abdomens to the surface.

Both males and females collapse to the water spent, sometimes in great numbers. PMD spinners fall in early morning or late evening. If you arrive at the stream just as the duns emerge and leave soon after they're done, you might never encounter a PMD spinnerfall.

Ginger Quill Spinner

Behavior and Tactics

Though PMD spinnerfalls might take place on gentle riffles or runs, you're almost certain to find trout feeding on them selectively on glides or flats. But never overlook them at the edges of riffles and runs or upstream and down where the water smoothes out and trout can set up stations and feed patiently on spinners trapped in the surface film. Use your lightest tackle and most delicate presentations. During PMD spinnerfalls, cross-stream reach casts and downstream wiggle casts will solve more situations for you than upstream casts that line the trout.

Known Hatches

Rather than taking a known hatch approach to the PMDs, expect to run into them in your summer travels, no matter where you go in the West. Always carry a small box full of flies dedicated just to the nymph, emerger, dun, and spinner stages of the PMDs.

Lesser Green Drake nymph

Common names: Lesser Green Drake nymph, Flav nymph, smaller *Drunella* nymph

Latin names: *Drunella flavilinea, D. coloradensis*

Size range: #12–14 (7–12 mm, ¼–½ inch excluding tails)

Key Features

Tails: Three, same length, with black band near center of each

Gills: Small and oval, on abdominal segments 3-7

Body shape: Stout; paired projections on back edge of each abdominal segment

Body color: Reddish to dark brown

Legs: Thick and strong; femurs have serrated front edges

Habitat

Nymphs of Lesser Green Drakes demand cool and clean water, flowing over rocky streambeds. They can be found in freestone streams, spring creeks, and tailwaters so long as flows are moderate to fast. Their populations are distributed in streams of all sizes, from small headwaters to the largest Western trout rivers. There is often confusion between *D. flavilinea* and *D. coloradensis* hatches; the same patterns will work for both.

Emergence

Lesser Green Drake nymphs get restless in the weeks before their summer and fall emergences, are found in the drift far more often, and are more likely to be taken selectively then. During the hatch, they leave the bottom and swim feebly to the top. Many are taken along the way or just beneath the surface. The nymphs are most important as models for imitation in the days just before a hatch or during the hatch itself.

Behavior and Tactics

Lesser Green Drake nymphs do not swim well. Their imitations should be fished dead-drift. In the days prior to hatches, and in the hours before the daily hatch, rig with indicator and shot, and fish the nymphs dead-drift along the bottom. When a hatch begins, before trout focus on floating duns, try rigging the nymph as a dropper off a large dry fly or with a yarn strike indicator and two to three feet of tippet. Fish the nymph as you would a dry, with a drag-free drift, but just a few inches deep.

Known Hatches

Fall R., OR; Logan R., UT; Frying Pan R., CO; Lamar R., WY; Yakima R., WA; Big Hole R., MT. It's likely that Lesser Green Drakes are often mistaken for the slightly larger Western Green Drakes, and that many hatches listed for the more famous insect are actually this one.

Lesser Green Drake dun

Lesser Green Drake dun

Common names: Lesser Green Drake dun, Flav dun, smaller *Drunella* dun

Latin names: *Drunella flavilinea, D. coloradensis*

Size range: #12–14 (7–13 mm, ⅜–⅝ inch excluding tails)

Key Features

Tails: Three

Body color: Dark olive on back, pale olive underside; lacks distinct banding

Forewings: Pale to dark gray

Hindwings: Moderate size; slightly rounded angle on leading edge

Habitat

Though the nymphs often live in broken water, they either migrate to calmer water for emergence or drift to smoother water before emerging. They emerge midwater, usually on flats or quiet edge waters near riffles and runs. They also emerge on quiet pools downstream from riffles and on benches in stairstep mountain streams. Trout get a good look at the big naturals, and the flies that match them.

Emergence

Seasonal emergence starts in June and July in the Pacific and Great Basin regions and in late August through September in the Rockies. Daily emergence begins in mid to late afternoon and lasts from half an hour on sunny days to two or three hours on cloudy or rainy days. The transition from nymph to dun takes place just beneath the surface or in it, and many duns have trouble separating themselves from their nymphal shucks. A cripple pattern will serve you well.

Behavior and Tactics

These big duns often attempt to fly but then fall back to the water. Sometimes they'll flutter a few inches over the surface. They often float for ten to twenty feet before lifting off. Rig with 4X tippets to balance the large imitations, but go to 5X if necessary to fool trout. On mountain streams you can get away with fishing upstream. On larger and smoother flats and glides, fish cross-stream or downstream. Always try a dead-drift float, but if that fails to move trout, skate the fly a few inches and then let it drift without movement.

Known Hatches

Fall R., OR; Logan R., UT; Frying Pan R., CO; Lamar R., WY; Yakima R., WA; Big Hole R., MT. I have fished over the Lesser Green Drake hatch, or collected its nymphs, on these waters, but you might encounter it on any cold, clear Western trout stream or river.

Lesser Green Drake spinner

Lesser Green Drake spinner (Jim Schollmeyer)

Common names: Lesser Green Drake spinner, Flav spinner, smaller *Drunella* spinner
Latin names: *Drunella flavilinea, D. coloradensis*
Size range: #12–14 (7–13 mm, ⅜–⅝ inch excluding tails)

Key Features

Tails: Three
Body color: Olive-brown to reddish brown
Forewings: Clear, glassy
Hindwings: Moderate size; slightly rounded angle on leading edge

Habitat

Lesser Green Drake spinnerfalls are important only where dun emergences are substantial. If the hatch is sparse, spinners will return to the water too sporadically to cause selective feeding. Where they're abundant, these spinners are so large that trout will not ignore them. They're usually taken in the smooth water of pools and glides just downstream from the faster water above which mating takes place.

Emergence

Males gather over the edges of the stream, or above riffles, usually at midmorning, though in warm weather it might happen in evening and on hot days it can get pushed to the following dawn. Females, and some males, fall to the water spent, often on water smooth enough to cause selectivity. It can be difficult to see them on the water; use your aquarium net to seine the surface currents.

CDC Rusty Spinner

Behavior and Tactics

When trout feed selectively on Lesser Green Drake spinners, the naturals will be trapped in the surface film. Trout usually take them with gentle sipping rises, though sometimes the size of the insect will prompt a bolder take. If fishing pressure is at all heavy, the trout will be a bit snotty. Your leader will have to be twelve to fourteen feet long, with at least three feet of 4X or 5X tippet. On lightly fished water, or water a bit rough, use upstream presentations. Everywhere else, fish across stream or downstream.

Known Hatches

Because these spinnerfalls often catch you by surprise, it's best to arm yourself with an imitation and be ready to fish it wherever and whenever you suddenly find the natural important to trout.

Western Green Drake nymph

Western Green Drake nymph

Key Features

Tails: Three, equal length, with whorls of short hairs
Gills: Plate-shaped, on abdominal segments 3-7 or 2-9
Body shape: Blocky; with prominent spines on abdomen and head*
Body color: Light to reddish to dark brown, almost black
Legs: Thick and strong

*Note: *Drunella doddsii* body is short and wide, lacks spines; underside has a suckerlike disk

Common names: Western Green Drake nymph, Lead-Winged Olive nymph
Latin names: *Drunella grandis, D. doddsii, D. spinifera*
Size range: #8–12 (14–16 mm, 5/8–3/4 inch excluding tails)

Habitat

Green Drake nymphs can be found anywhere from mountain streams to mature rivers, from freestone streams to spring creeks and tailwaters. They require clean, cold flows. They're most common in streams with bouldered beds and prefer larger rock over pebbled or cobbled bottoms. But they have also adapted to systems with rooted vegetation, notably the heavy Western Green Drake hatch on the Railroad Ranch section of the Henrys Fork of the Snake River.

Emergence

These big nymphs do their dun stage a favor by migrating out of violent water before emerging. On rivers such as the Big Hole, Madison, and Deschutes, you can often do well by dead-drifting a nymph near the banks in the days before the hatch. Other times, the nymphs remain in fast water, in the fastest parts of riffles broken by big stones, and the duns release there. A nymph dressing based on them is almost always a good bet for the larger fly in a two-nymph combination, fished on the bottom in moderate to big water.

Behavior and Tactics

These big, blocky nymphs are poor swimmers. They live in currents that are often brutal, and they're often knocked loose and tumbled into the drift. When they are, they're unable to do much more than wiggle uselessly until their own density delivers them back to the bottom or to a waiting trout. Your imitations should be rigged for the indicator-and-shot method on big water. Dispense with the shot and use a weighted imitation beneath a yarn indicator on small streams. Always fish them on or near the bottom with a dead-drift presentation.

Known Hatches

Deschutes R., OR; Yakima R., WA; Skagit R., BC; Bow R., AB; Henrys Fork and South Fork Snake R., ID; Big Hole R., Madison R., and Yellowstone R., MT; Green R., WY; Green R., UT. There are many lesser-known but important Green Drake hatches.

Western Green Drake dun

Western Green Drake dun

Common names: Western Green Drake dun, Lead-Winged Olive
Latin names: *Drunella grandis, D. doddsii, D. spinifera*
Size range: #8–12 (13–16 mm, 7⁄16–3⁄4 inch excluding tails)

Key Features

Tails: Three
Body color: Bright to dark green, with distinct banding
Forewings: Large, medium to slate gray
Hindwings: Modest size; distinct, rounded angle on leading edge

Habitat

Most famous Western Green Drake hatches take place on flat water. Those from rough water release from the bottom at the upper ends of pools, where heavy flows roll over big boulders; then the duns appear on the surface ten to twenty feet downstream, where the water has calmed a bit. Many also hatch in softer edge currents alongside riffles and runs or on fairly smooth runs in big freestone rivers.

Emergence

Green Drakes emerge in late May, June, and July on the coast and in the Great Basin, and in August and early September in the Rockies and north. Daily emergence begins in late morning or early afternoon and lasts from half an hour to three hours. In a few famous places the hatch is heavy. On most waters it could be described as trickling, with an occasional dun drifting on the water. Even a very sparse hatch will get trout up and interested.

Behavior and Tactics

These big insects have trouble escaping their nymphal shucks and getting airborne. A cripple dressing fished dead-drift can be very effective. The dun, once out of the nymph shuck, struggles on the surface, sometimes for several feet, making two or three attempts at liftoff before one is successful. Most of the time, trout will accept a dead-drifted dry fly, but if they refuse it, position yourself to skate the fly slightly and then let it sit. I have done experiments fishing Mike Lawson's Paradrake alongside less imitative patterns. It always wins.

Known Hatches

If you time it right, you can get into one of the famous heavy Green Drake hatches. Most of the time, you'll get into a sporadic hatch, and you'll have to watch for occasional rising trout. They'll be glad to get that big imitation, wherever you find them.

Western Green Drake spinner

Western Green Drake spinner

Common names: Western Green Drake spinner, Lead-Winged Olive spinner

Latin names: *Drunella grandis, D. doddsii, D. spinifera*

Size range: #8–12 (13–16 mm, 7/16–3/4 inch excluding tails)

Key Features

Tails: Three

Body color: Reddish brown to dark brown, with distinct banding

Forewings: Large, clear, glassy

Hindwings: Modest size; distinct, rounded angle on leading edge

Habitat

Green Drake spinner flights are rarely important except on waters with heavy hatches. The flight might form over any part of the stream, but the spinnerfall itself will usually be on the gentle surface of a pool or on a glide or flat. If the naturals deposit their eggs in a riffle or run, trout will usually gather downstream to feed on the trapped naturals in smoother water.

Emergence

It's been reported that Western Green Drake spinners make their mating flights in the evening, but the females return to vegetation to let their eggs become fertilized overnight and lay their eggs in the earliest hours of the morning. I haven't often observed falls of these big spinners heavy enough to cause trout to rise selectively, but I might have missed them by sleeping in. It doesn't take many of these large spinners to interest trout.

Behavior and Tactics

After they lay their eggs, the big spinners fall to the water spent, with their wings outspread. Trout know they are not going anywhere, and feed gracefully and patiently on them. Your rig should be as delicate as you can make it to handle such large flies; 4X and 5X tippets will be necessary. If the water is slightly rumpled, as in a riffle or run, then position yourself to make upstream casts, avoiding those straight upstream that line the trout. If the water is smooth and the trout skittish, use a cross-stream reach cast or downstream wiggle cast.

Known Hatches

Such big Western rivers as the Bighorn, Madison, Big Hole, Bow, Henrys Fork, and Deschutes all have fishable spinnerfalls of the Western Green Drakes. But many lesser-known waters will surprise you with them as well.

Great Red Quill dun

Great Red Quill dun

Key Features

Tails: Three
Body color: Olive to olive-brown
Abdomen: Segments 8 and 9 with projections on sides
Forewings: Medium to slate gray
Hindwings: Moderate size; rounded projection on leading edge

Common names: *Timpanoga*, Great Red Quill dun, Great Blue-Winged Red Quill dun, Western Green Drake dun
Latin names: *Timpanoga hecuba hecuba* and *T. hecuba pacifica*
Size range: #8–12 (15–17 mm, 5⁄8–3⁄4 inch excluding tails)

Habitat

Timpanoga nymphs have operculate gills: the front gill is a plate that lifts to expose the others to aquatic oxygen. They're able to thrive in streams where irrigation return, glacial melt, or thunderstorms add silt to the system. They're often the most important mayfly where others survive in low numbers. The nymphs are not fed upon selectively, but the duns are often the cause of significant rises.

Emergence

Seasonal emergence is mid-July to mid-August in coastal and lowland regions, and late August though mid-September on inland streams and at higher elevations. Daily emergence begins in early to midafternoon and can go on for two to three hours on cloudy or rainy days. These big duns leave the nymphal shuck beneath the surface and have trouble getting through the surface film. They often ride gentle currents for several feet, fluttering often, before they're able to fly.

Behavior and Tactics

These large olive-brown insects are related to, and often mistaken for, Western Green Drakes. Trout make the same mistake; you can fish them with the same dressings. Because they have trouble getting off the water, a cripple is often better than a floating dun pattern. The same set of tactics used for Green Drakes will work as well. You'll usually find them emerging on gentle water downstream from riffles. If the water and trout allow it, fish with upstream presentations. If not, use the cross-stream reach or downstream wiggle.

Known Hatches

The Lamar River, Slough Creek, and Soda Butte Creek in Yellowstone Park are all known for *Timpanoga*, because of silt loads from thunderstorms. But these duns are important in many scattered, isolated, and little-known streams affected by glacial melt or irrigation return.

Small Blue-Winged Olive nymph

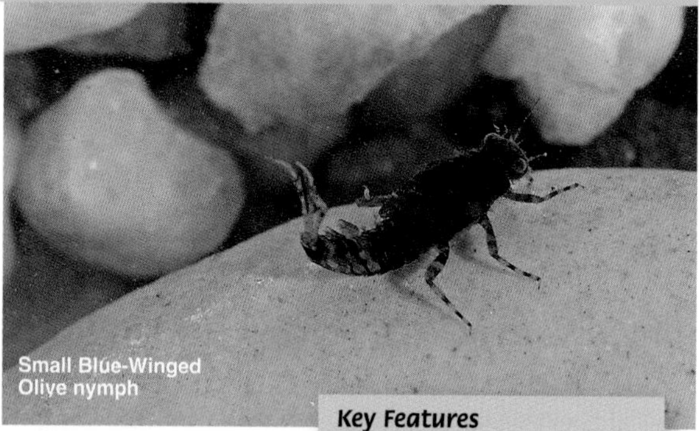

Common names: Small Blue-Winged Olive, margarita nymph
Latin name: *Attenella margarita*
Size range: #16–18 (6–9 mm, 5⁄16–3⁄8 inch)

Key Features

Tails: Three, covered with fine hairs
Body: Paired small projections on each abdominal segment
Color: Light amber to dark brown; segments 4, 5, and 8 often pale
Gills: Platelike, on segments 4-7

Habitat

These small crawler nymphs prefer slow to moderate currents and are collected most often where scour is modest and some vegetation is able to take root on the bottom. They crawl clumsily among the rocks or in the plants. I have collected them in greatest numbers by sweeping a net through trailing vegetation in slow currents. Though they do get into the drift, they are by far most important during a hatch.

Emergence

Seasonal emergence is triggered by water temperatures approaching 50 degrees F., generally in July in the western parts of their range, in August through September in the Rockies. Daily hatches begin at around 9:00 a.m. and on cloudy days last until noon. They hatch in smooth flows or mild edge currents. Though you'll notice duns, and trout feeding on them, it's probable that for every dun that goes down, eight to ten nymphs are taken on their way up.

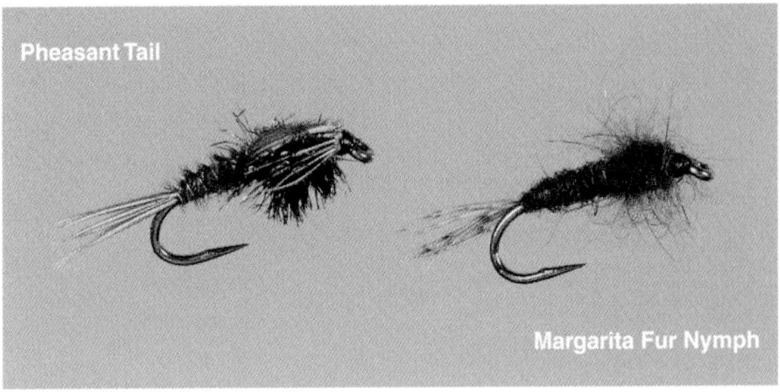

Behavior and Tactics

John Juracek and Craig Mathews, in *Fishing Yellowstone Hatches*, report trout feeding visibly on these nymphs in the Yellowstone River in the park. They advise spotting trout and presenting the fly a few inches to a foot deep. Rig with a long 5X or 6X tippet, and add a small indicator to detect takes. Present the nymph upstream to feeding trout just as you would fish a dry fly. If trout are not visible, rig the same way and fish the nymph, or pair of them, under the emerging duns.

Known Hatches

Hat Ck., CA; Tygh Ck., OR; Henrys Fork Snake R., ID; Big Hole R., MT; Yellowstone R., WY. It's certain that this small insect is underreported and much more widespread.

Small Blue-Winged Olive dun

Small Blue-Winged Olive dun

Common names:
Small Blue-Winged Olive, margarita dun
Latin name: *Attenella margarita*
Size range: #16–18
(6–8 mm, 5⁄16–3⁄8 inch)

Key Features

Tails: Three
Body: Bright to medium olive or olive-brown
Forewings: Medium gray
Hindwings: Prominent; slightly rounded angle on leading edge

Habitat

I have found these small olives hatching most often on quiet currents: spring creeks, tailwaters, lowland streams with flows reduced by irrigation demands, or the side currents of large freestone rivers. I have found them in scant numbers in more boisterous riffles and runs, but have never found trout feeding selectively on them there. In freestone waters, they're usually most important in edge currents.

Emergence

Annual emergence is in midsummer on the coast and at lower elevations. Their most important hatches are in late August and September in the higher Rocky Mountain areas. They are a morning hatch, lasting an hour or two between nine and noon on most days. Duns are reported to emerge from the nymph beneath the surface. The small olive, or *margarita* as it is often called, is subject to a high rate of cripples.

Behavior and Tactics

Small Blue-Winged Olive duns struggle through the film and then sit for some time while their wings dry, with an occasional flutter that is an early attempt at flight. Trout generally set up in quiet currents and sip the duns gently, though it's wise to remember that surface feeding is most likely no more than the visible tip of the iceberg; more are taken as nymphs. Consider suspending a nymph pattern under your dry. Rig with long and fine tippets, and use presentations demanded of smooth flows: either cross-stream reach casts or downstream wiggle casts.

Known Hatches

Notice the few known hatches listed for the nymph stage. The small Blue-Winged Olive dun is so similar in size, shape, and shared habitat to the more common Blue-Winged Olive (*Baetis*) that it's almost certain we've all fished over it and not known it.

Mahogany dun

Mahogany dun

Common names: Mahogany dun, Red Quill, Iron Blue dun
Latin name: *Paraleptophlebia* (25 related Western species)
Size range: #12–18 (6–12 mm, ¼–½ inch, excluding tails)

Key Features

Tails: Three, equal in length
Body color: Underside tan to reddish brown; some pale gray
Abdomen: Usually long and slender
Forewings: Smokey gray
Hindwings: Modest size, oval

Habitat

Mahogany nymphs are crawlers, but not robust. They're found more often in small to medium-sized streams than large rivers, though hatches can be important along the edges of some big waters. The nymphs live in leaf packs and woody debris in quiet water, and trout do not feed on them selectively. Duns almost always emerge along the banks, where they drift in quiet lines, or in eddies, while trout sip them.

Emergence

Seasonal hatches are in spring, April and May, or fall, September and early October, separated by species rather than geography.

You'll find spring and fall hatches in both Pacific and Rockies regions. Daily emergence begins in late morning or early afternoon to midafternoon, and it lasts two or three hours except on sunny days. Emergence takes place in the surface film. Duns usually ride the currents for several feet, sitting placidly without movement while their wings dry.

Behavior and Tactics

You'll almost always find these duns riding smooth edge currents or eddies, though they sometimes hatch on the broad weedy flats of spring creek and tailwater flows. Trout usually sip them patiently. You need to pinpoint the lie of a rising trout, move into position to put as many conflicting currents behind you as you can, and present your imitation without lining the fish. You'll often be on the bank, casting to trout rising very near it. If you're forced to fish upstream, use a long, fine tippet, and avoid casting over the head of the trout.

Known Hatches

Clark Fork of the Columbia R., MT; Henrys Fork Snake R., ID; Yellowstone R., WY; Deschutes R., OR. These are large rivers with known hatches; you might find Mahoganies on any Western stream or river. Because they're tucked so near the edges, they're often overlooked.

Mahogany spinner

Mahogany spinner (Jim Schollmeyer)

Common names: Red Quill, Blue Quill
Latin name: *Paraleptophlebia* (25 related Western species)
Size range: #12–18 (6–12 mm, ¼–½ inch, excluding tails)

Key Features

Tails: Three, equal in length
Body color: Females, reddish to purplish brown or gray; males, white or clear with dark brown tip
Forewings: Clear, sometimes with amber tint
Hindwings: Modest size, oval

Habitat

Spinner flights of Mahoganies form above the banks of the same streams from which the duns emerged, often so late they're almost impossible to notice. If hatches are modest to light, spinnerfalls will not be important. The spinners often fall to the surfaces of flats and pools and along quiet edges. They're often the cause of subtle, sipping rises that occur on smooth flats and tailouts just before dark.

Emergence

Seasonal spinnerfalls come on the tails of spring and fall dun emergences. They are most important in April and May, seldom important through the summer, and important once again in September and October. Daily falls are most often just at evening, as it begins to get too dark to see what is on the water. Use your aquarium net to seine the surface currents. You might need a flashlight to see the slight spinners you've collected.

Behavior and Tactics

Trout sipping Mahogany spinners are almost always working smooth currents. If you get into an evening rise to something invisible, suspect spinners—if not Mahoganies, something similar. Try to collect a specimen of what the trout are taking. If you can't, try a size 14 or 16 Red Quill Spinner. Rig for delicacy, and put your fly over the rising trout without lining them. You aren't likely to be able to see your fly. If necessary, add a yarn indicator to the leader five or six feet above it.

Known Hatches

Rather than thinking in terms of famous hatches, tie a small box of Red Quill and Blue Quill Spinners, and carry them wherever you go. The key to spinner fishing, Mahoganies or otherwise, is to be on the water in late afternoon and evening, sometimes right up until dark.

Trico dun

Common names: Trico, White-Winged Curse, Snowflake Mayfly

Latin names: *Tricorythodes explicatus* (was *T. fallax, T. minutus*); *Asioplax edmunsi* (was *Tricorythodes edmunsi*)

Size range: #18–24 (3–6 mm, ⅛–¼ inch excluding tails)

Key Features

Tails: Three; females, short; males, long

Size: Very small; thorax stocky

Body color: Females, pale green with brown thorax; males, brown abdomen and thorax

Forewings: Pale whitish gray

Hindwings: Absent

Habitat

Trico nymphs live in slow currents in small streams to large rivers. They do well in silted waters, though they're also found in clean systems. They inhabit plant beds and are also found where rocks are coated with algae and diatoms. Tricos hatch in pastoral streams with irrigation return, but also in spring creeks and large tailwaters, and in some large and small rivers systems where farming is a factor.

Emergence

Tricos can hatch between June and October but are heaviest in late July through August and into early September. Daily emergence is split, with the males emerging in late afternoon and evening, and females hatching in early morning. Though many crawl out of the water to emerge, trout find plenty emerging out in open water, normally near the edges. You can find trout sipping male duns close to dark or feeding selectively on female duns in the first few hours of daylight.

Behavior and Tactics

On spring creek and tailwater flats, Tricos emerge in open water. On all other waters they emerge within a few feet of the shoreline. Those that crawl out on rocks and grasses are often blown to the water an inch or two from the bank, where trout sip them quietly. Refine your tippet to three or four feet of 6X or 7X. You can fish from downstream, off to the side, or upstream, but you'll have to place your tiny imitation precisely in the trout's feeding lane, just when it's ready to rise for another natural.

Known Hatches

Bow R., AB; Missouri R., Big Hole R., Bighorn R., Yellowstone valley spring creeks, Madison Arm of Hebgen Lake, MT; Henrys Fork Snake R. and Silver Ck., ID; Madison R. in Yellowstone Park, WY; many gentle reaches of streams that are unknown or little-known.

Trico spinner

Trico male (left) and female (right) spinners

Common names: Trico, White-Winged Curse, Snowflake Mayfly
Latin names: *Tricorythodes explicatus* (was *T. fallax, T. minutus*); *Asioplax edmunsi* (was *Tricorythodes edmunsi*)
Size range: #18–24 (3–6 mm, ⅛–¼ inch excluding tails)

Key Features

Tails: Three, body length to twice body length
Size: Very small; thorax stocky
Body color: Females, olive abdomen, dark brown thorax, often with black egg mass; males, brown abdomen, black thorax
Forewings: Clear, glassy
Hindwings: Absent

Habitat

The spinner is the most important stage of the Trico. Flights form along the edges, often towering in great masses. Even on waters where duns emerge unnoticed, enough spinners can gather to cause selective feeding. Spinners fall to the water on placid edge currents, usually within five to fifteen feet from the bank. Back-channel flows behind islands are favorable places to find trout rising to sip them.

Emergence

Seasonal spinnerfalls occur in July, August, and September. They gather in the air as early as 8:00 a.m., and as late as 10:00 a.m. Usually the spinners mass and tower for some time and then all collapse to the water at the same time. The water can be covered with their spent bodies. Trout sip, or sometimes get greedy, gulping them as fast as they can. It can be incredibly difficult fishing; I often mismatch the hatch with a Pale Morning Dun or small caddis imitation. Often a sunk soft-hackle is better than a dry fly. Experiment!

Behavior and Tactics

Tricos fall to the water spent, typically massed on the water. Trout feed on them in eager pods, working slowly upstream for twenty to fifty feet and then circling downstream to their original position and working upstream again. They remain high in the water between takes. Use cross-stream or downstream casts, and present the fly precisely in front of a trout just when it's ready to take another natural. Watch carefully to see if trout feed on the surface or just beneath it. If a dry imitation fails, try swinging the Soft-Hackle Trico Spinner or mismatching the hatch.

Known Hatches

Famous spinnerfalls are on the same waters as those listed for duns. But be on the watch for Tricos on waters of all sizes. The key is to be on the water in the morning and to watch for the gathering spinners.

Western March Brown nymph

Common name: Western March Brown nymph
Latin names: *Rhithrogena morrisoni, R. hageni*
Size range: #12–16 (5–12 mm, ¼–½ inch excluding tails)

Key Features

Tails: Three, body length or shorter; usually white
Gills: Large; form suckerlike disc on underside of abdomen
Body shape: Flattened; head equal in width to thorax
Body color: Olive-brown to reddish brown
Eyes: Embedded in top of head

Habitat

Western March Brown nymphs are clingers adapted to fast water. They're most common in medium to large rivers. Prior to emergence they migrate upstream or down to the calmer water of broad runs and flats, so imitations are usually fished on smooth flows. They're most important in the early hours of a hatch, when trout often focus selectively on nymphs just subsurface as opposed to duns floating on top.

Emergence

Seasonal emergence begins in February in the lowlands, peaks in March, and tapers off in April. At higher elevations, it begins in May and continues through June and July. Daily emergence usually starts in early afternoon and lasts an hour or two, or longer on rainy days. The nymphs gather in great numbers on flats downstream from riffles in the days before an emergence. Emergence itself takes place on smooth water, not fast water.

Behavior and Tactics

March Brown nymphs leave the bottom, swim almost to the surface, and shed the nymphal shuck either just beneath or in the surface film. Arlen Thomason, in *BugWater*, reports observing them making several attempts to break through the film before finally emerging. Trout focus on nymphs in the early stages of a hatch. Some trout feed on nymphs through the hatch. Fish your nymph inches deep, on a dead drift, just as you would a dry fly.

Known Hatches

McKenzie R., Willamette R., and Deschutes R., OR; Yakima R., WA; Henrys Fork Snake R., ID; Bitterroot R., MT. This is a short list of places where I have fished heavy hatches of March Browns. They're very widespread and important on many other Western rivers.

Western March Brown dun

Western March Brown dun

Common name: Western March Brown dun
Latin names: *Rhithrogena morrisoni, R. hageni*
Size range: #12–16 (5–15 mm, ¼–⅝ inch excluding tails)

Key Features

Tails: Two, about body length, white
Body color: Back, light to reddish brown; underside, olive-tan to light brown
Forewings: Large, mottled brown and black; dark area on upper leading edge
Hindwings: Large, oval; angle in leading edge
Head: Retains wide, flat aspect of nymph

Habitat

The best hatches of March Brown duns are on smooth runs and flats, most often on broad stretches of large, mature freestone rivers. They're important in tailwaters with riffled freestone reaches, such as the big and brawling Deschutes River. The only spring creek in which I've fished them is the Henrys Fork, and it receives only half of its water from springs; the other half is from a tailwater source.

Emergence

The March Brown is the first hatch of large mayflies in the Western season, before spring runoff. Seasonal emergence is in February, March, and April in low areas, and in April, May, and June at higher elevations. Daily hatches begin when the water warms, sometimes in late morning, more often in early to late afternoon. As with most mayflies, the hatch might be short on sunny days but will go on for two or three hours under clouds and in the rain.

Behavior and Tactics

Though March Brown duns arise from nymphs adapted to fast water, you'll need dun imitations that fish best on glides and flats. I've fished collar-hackled traditional patterns against parachutes and Compara-duns that lower the body of the imitation into the surface film, and I have caught almost no trout with standard hackled patterns. Your rigging should be suitable to smooth water, with light lines and 3-foot 4X or 5X tippets. Presentations should be cross-stream or downstream on all but wrinkled water. You won't do well if you line trout sipping March Brown duns.

Known Hatches

The same as those listed for nymphs. Last year I fished the Deschutes River in April. The first day it rained; the hatch was excellent. The second day the sun shone; the hatch was brief and sparse. The third day it poured, and the hatch was the heaviest I've ever fished.

Pale Evening Dun

Pale Evening Dun

Common names: Pale Evening Dun, Western Ginger Quill, Western Light Cahill
Latin name: *Heptagenia elegantula* (3 related Western species)
Size range: #12–16 (5–15 mm, ¼–⅝ inch excluding tails)

Key Features

Tails: Two, about body length
Body color: Creamish white to pale yellow
Forewings: Large; pale cream to light tan
Hindwings: Large; sharp angle on leading edge
Head: Retains flattened aspect of clinger nymph

Habitat

Pale Evening Dun nymphs are clingers, but they typically live in moderate or even slow flows, rather than riffles, of medium to large trout rivers. They can be found in both freestone streams and tailwaters but are rarely important in spring creeks. The duns almost always drift in modest currents along the edges, or at least near the shores, of sizable stream and river systems.

Emergence

Hatches begin in late May and June on the coast and continue through August and September in the Rockies. Daily emergence is in late afternoon to late evening, sometimes lasting until dark or after. The nymphs migrate to shallow and slow water at the edges of riffles, runs, and freestone flats. Emergence from the nymphal cuticle takes place on the bottom. The dun, not the nymph, swims awkwardly to the surface and is important to imitate.

Behavior and Tactics

Because the dun emerges on the bottom and swims to the top, in calm edge flows, you'll often do well with a wet fly. A wet is useful only on waters where you're able to wade away from the bank and cast back to it. If you see trout feeding on floating duns within a foot to ten feet from the bank, then switch to the floating pattern, and fish it with a method suitable to the type of surface: upstream if it's a bit rough, cross-stream or downstream if it's smooth.

Known Hatches

To list specific hatches would do the Pale Evening Dun a disservice; I've found it on nearly all Western streams and rivers of more than average size. The key is to be on the stream late, after it seems the fishing has ended for the day.

Pale Evening Dun spinner

Pale Evening Dun spinner

Common names: Pale Evening Dun spinner, Western Ginger Quill spinner

Latin name: *Heptagenia elegantula* (3 related Western species)

Size range: #12–16 (5–15 mm, ¼–⅝ inch excluding tails)

Key Features

Tails: Two, body length or longer

Body color: Female, creamish white to pale yellow; male, red-brown

Forewings: Large; clear, glassy

Hindwings: Large; sharp angle on leading edge

Habitat

Pale Evening Dun spinner flights gather above the stream banks in late afternoon and early evening. It's important to know that the flight itself contains almost all males, which are reddish brown, but that trout feed almost exclusively on females, which are pale yellow. Females lay their eggs at the lower ends or calmer edges of riffles, or on the surfaces of pools, usually as light is beginning to fail.

Emergence

Your tipoff to an important evening spinner flight is an emergence of duns on the same day or the day before. Seasonally, this will be any time from late May through mid-September. Daily might be in late afternoon on cloudy days, but more often at dusk, lasting right up until dark. It's an easy spinnerfall to miss if you leave the stream for the normal dinner hour in camp or at the lodge.

Western Ginger Quill Spinner

Behavior and Tactics

Pale Evening Dun spinners fall to the water spent. Though they're not difficult to notice in the air, they're almost impossible to notice on the water. They're the frequent cause of selective feeding by trout just before dark. It can be very frustrating until you take time to suspend your aquarium net in the surface currents and hold it there for a fair length of time. Then you might need a headlamp to get a good look at the fragile spinners in the meshes. Match them with Ginger Quill Spinners, and fish them with fine gear and delicate presentations.

Known Hatches

Almost all Western streams and rivers have at least minor hatches of Pale Evening Duns. But only those with heavy hatches have important spinnerfalls. You'll rarely notice them if you're not on the water in late evening.

Brown Drake dun

Common name: Brown Drake
Latin name: *Ephemera simulans*
Size range: #8–12 (15–20 mm, ½–¾ inch excluding tails)

Key Features

Tails: Three
Body color: Yellowish tan to brown with dark markings
Forewings: Large, mottled
Hindwings: Large, oval; rounded leading edge

Habitat

Brown Drake nymphs are burrowers. They need bottoms of fine gravel, sand, or silt in which they can conceal themselves. They're found in meadow stream reaches where such material settles. They're not found in freestone streams with typical bottom compositions of rocks and boulders. Their populations are scattered throughout the West. Because of their large size, trout key on Brown Drake duns whenever they get a chance at them.

Emergence

Hatches begin in late June, extending through July and into early August. In a few waters at high altitude, Brown Drakes emerge in September. Daily emergence might begin in late afternoon on rare days with heavy cloud cover, but most of the time they hatch just before and after dark. Nymphs pause just beneath the surface, and the dun emerges there. Duns finish the trip through the surface film quickly and leave the water after just a short float.

Brown Paradrake

Behavior and Tactics

These big duns are not on the water long, and it's dark, or almost so, when they get there. But they're so large that trout get greedy about them. The largest trout in any stretch of river will feed on Brown Drake duns and not be leader-shy. Use a 3X tippet. Make your casts upstream, but if trout refuse you, move into position to fish across or even downstream. Some of the waters where Brown Drakes emerge are heavily fished, and the trout are far from foolish, despite their lack of awareness of leaders.

Known Hatches

Bow R. and Red Deer R., AB; Yellowstone R., Madison R., and Missouri R., MT; Green R. and Encampment R., WY; Green R., UT. The most important Brown Drake hatches run through the Rocky Mountain provinces and states, becoming less important as you go west.

6 Stoneflies

Stoneflies important to anglers in the West break down quite differently from mayflies. In their smaller sizes, 14 to 18, they split into three color themes that are repeated consistently throughout almost all Western waters: the Little Brown Stones, Little Green Stones, and Little Yellow Stones. The two latter groups are referred to more often as *Olive Sallies* and *Yellow Sallies*, nomenclature I will follow in this book. The larger stoneflies also break down into three specific types to which you need to give your attention: Skwalas, Golden Stones, and the famous Salmonfly.

The smaller groups do not lend themselves to understanding by species, or even by genus, as do the mayflies. The Little Brown Stones alone comprise four families, more genera than I care to count, and a true confusion of individual species. You could spend a fly-fishing career sorting them out. Just when you had them sorted, taxonomists would change classifications and toss all your work into the air. In the end, you would fish them all with one or two fly patterns. By learning to recognize a Little Brown Stone at a glance, and by knowing which pattern to tie on to match it, you'll do as well as somebody who has learned to identify it to species. You might do better: you spent your time honing your fishing skills while he spent his peering through microscopes.

The same is true for Olive and Yellow Sallies: You'll gain a lot by learning to recognize them, and match them, but you won't add much more to your success by studying their peripheral parts so you can key them to family, genus, and species.

The larger stoneflies are less complex, taxonomically, so that when you've learned to recognize them by their key characteristics,

Little Brown Stone nymphs, and Olive Sally nymphs as well, are small, and not often found in such concentrated numbers that trout feed on them selectively. You rarely need to tie flies specifically to imitate them. Instead, try generic nymphs such as the Pheasant Tail, Copper John, or small Gold-Ribbed Hare's Ears. They'll almost always work.

Salmonfly nymphs are so large, and when migrating for emergence gather in such masses under rocks along the shoreline, that trout feed on them selectively, and they must be matched.

you've come closer to determining their genus and species. Salmonflies, for example, arrive almost everywhere in the single species *Pteronarcys californica*. A less common species overlaps with it, and I've collected it in a few headwater streams, but they're so similar I didn't know it was a different species until I looked at it under a microscope. It's well known that trout don't own microscopes.

Golden Stones come in four species, in three separate genera, but it's academic; they're all so similar that the same set of flies fish for the nymphs and adults of all of them. *Skwala*, though I separate them out because their habitat and hatch season are different from those of Golden Stones, are similar enough in appearance that you could use the same patterns tied a bit smaller and trout wouldn't notice you'd tricked them.

LIFE CYCLE

Stoneflies need lots of oxygen and live only in flowing water, though a few species have been collected along wave-washed and therefore oxygenated shorelines of lakes. They're important in creeks, rivers, and streams, and are associated most often with the broken water of riffles, pocketwater, and choppy runs. Cold water entrains more oxygen than warmer water; stoneflies thrive in the kinds of water temperatures that trout prefer.

Stoneflies have *incomplete metamorphosis*. They have just two stages: nymph and adult. The winged adult closely resembles the mature nymph, in which the wings are accordioned in wing cases held on top of the last two thoracic segments. Emergence is always accomplished by crawling out of the water. It never occurs in open water, though an egg-depositing flight over a riffle, run, or flat can give the appearance of a hatch. Nymphs migrate to the shoreline or to protruding boulders along the edges. Then they crawl up through the waterline and emerge into adults a few inches to fifty feet from the water. This usually takes place at night, as a defense against bird predation, though you'll sometimes observe stoneflies emerging on cloudy afternoons. The nymph skin splits along the back, the adult slowly emerges, its wings pump up and dry out, and the adult walks away from its abandoned shuck.

Stoneflies have incomplete metamorphosis: the nymph is shaped very much like the adult. The maturing wings are carried in wing cases on the second and third thoracic segments. When the adult emerges, these wings are unfolded, and that is the largest difference between the nymph and adult . . . except that one lives beneath the water, the other in the aerial world.

Above: The largest and most important stonefly adults, Golden Stones and Salmonflies, mate in streamside vegetation, often on leaves that overhang water. They're clumsy climbers and frequently fall to water, to the delight of the trout.

All stoneflies crawl out to emerge. You don't fish a stonefly *hatch* as such. Imitate the nymphs during their migration toward shore; fish adult dressings along the edges when big stoneflies are hanging around, falling in, and getting eaten by trout; fish floating patterns over open water during egg-depositing flights.

Mating takes place in streamside vegetation, not in the air. The adults return to the water to lay their eggs, often in trickles, but sometimes in such great numbers that trout key on them. Such selective feeding is the criteria for imitation in both the nymph and adult stages.

The smallest groups, Little Brown Stones and Olive Sallies, do not migrate in sufficient numbers, in my experience, to cause selective feeding to the nymphal stage, but do fall to the water in enough densities to be fed on selectively as adults. All of the others, from Yellow Sallies through Skwala, Golden Stones, and Salmonflies, are fed on selectively in both nymph and adult stages, and you need imitations of them to successfully fish the wide array of Western waters.

Little Brown Stone adult

Common names: Little Brown Stone, Needle Fly, Winter Black, Little Red Stone

Latin names: Nemouridae, Leuctridae, Capniidae, Taeniopterygidae

Size range: #14–18 (7–13 mm, ¼–½ inch excluding tails)

Key Features

Tails: Two, from short, almost invisible, to long

Body shape: Slender, elongated, with little taper

Body color: Dark reddish brown to black

Wings: Held flat over back, extend beyond body, sometimes rolled

Antennae: Two, prominent, easily seen

Habitat

Most species in the Little Brown Stone group of families hatch from headwaters and streams of moderate size. They live only in cool flows that are well-oxygenated. Selectivity in such circumstances is less common than it is on slower water, farther down river systems. The nymphs themselves rarely gather in such numbers that trout focus on them. Adults occasionally buzz across the surface, laying eggs, in sufficient numbers to cause selective feeding.

Emergence

Most Little Brown Stones emerge February through April, though a few also hatch in early summer or fall. The main important period is before runoff begins. Daily hatch times are less important than the timing of egg laying, which will commonly be during the warmest parts of the day. In my own experience, the adults work edge currents, sometimes appearing on the water by crawling to it from shore rather than flying to it out of vegetation.

Behavior and Tactics

Most Little Brown Stone adults on the water aren't happy about being there. They're females, laying eggs, and seem intent on getting it done and getting out of there. They whir their wings so madly that they appear only a blur. Many species extrude a white egg mass and scurry at random on the water until it's dislodged. When you find trout taking Little Brown Stones selectively, try them first with the more imitative winged pattern, but if it fails, try skating the buzzer and then letting it drift. It might move trout that ignore a dead drift.

Known Hatches

Populations of Little Brown Stones can be collected in nearly every Western stream of small to modest size and in a few large rivers as well. They're only important where hatches are heavy and where streams are open to fishing in late winter and early spring.

Olive Sally adult

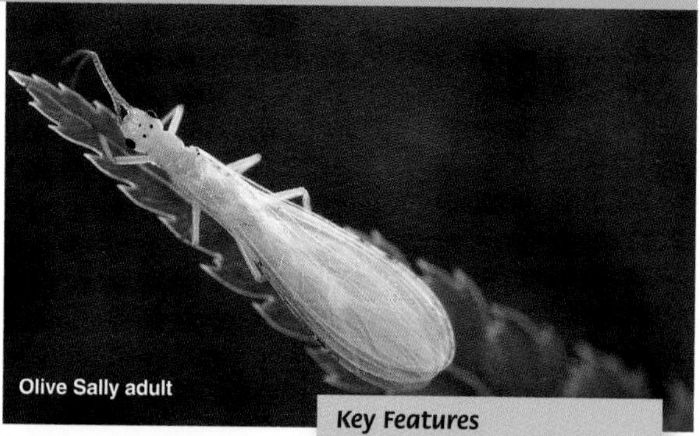

Olive Sally adult

Common names: Olive Sally, Little Green Stone, Olive Sallfly
Latin name: Chloroperlidae *Alloperla* (8 Western species)
Size range: #14–18 (10–13 mm, 3/8–1/2 inch excluding tails)

Key Features

Tails: Two, about half length of abdomen
Body shape: Slender, with little taper
Body color: Pale green to olive-yellow
Wings: Pale green to olive-yellow
Antennae: Prominent, easily seen

Habitat

Olive Sallies are found primarily in headwater streams. They are distributed all across the West, but are most important in the Rocky, Sierra, Cascade, and Coastal Mountain ranges. Nymphs are of little importance in terms of imitation. They live in leaf packs or hide deep in the gravel of riffles and runs. The adults are important when they return to the water to lay their eggs.

Emergence

Seasonal emergence begins in late April and May, is heaviest in June and July, and tapers off at lower altitudes in August and September, but it might be most important in those late summer months at higher elevations. Olive Sallies crawl out to emerge; daily hatch time is not important. But they become active and return to the water to lay their eggs in late afternoon and early evening. That is the most likely time to find trout feeding on Olive Sallies selectively.

Behavior and Tactics

Olive Sally females erupt out of streamside vegetation in late afternoon and evening, sometimes in great numbers. They descend over riffles and pools of small to medium mountain streams, and dip their abdomens to the surface to wash away their egg sacs. They're taken by trout either on the surface, or just as often beneath it, after they've collapsed to the water. On small water, too narrow to wade across, you'll usually be forced to fish with upstream casts, whether you fish the wet Partridge & Green or the floating Olive Sally. Both will work.

Known Hatches

Waters where Olive Sallies are important are rarely big enough to be known. If you fish any headwater areas of river systems, in any Western mountains, or have plans to, tie a few of the listed dressings and carry them with you for those moments when you need them.

Yellow Sally nymph

Yellow Sally nymphs

Common names: Yellow Sally nymph, Little Yellow Stone nymph, Yellow Sallfly nymph
Latin names: Perlodidae *Isoperla* (27 Western species); Chloroperlidae *Suwallia* (12) and *Sweltsa* (23)
Size range: #12–16 (7–22 mm, ¼–⅞ inch excluding tails)

Key Features

Tails: Two, about body length, stout
Body shape: Elongated; with little taper
Body color: Yellow to brown, often with black bands or stripes
Wing cases: Two pairs; distinct
Antennae: Prominent; easily seen

Habitat

The only requirement common to this large group of nymphs is clean, cold, flowing water. They might be abundant in anything from a tiny headwater stream to a mature valley river. Many are predaceous, feeding on midge and blackfly larvae, small mayflies, and caddis. They prowl and hunt in gravel and cobble bottoms of riffles and runs. They are found in freestone streams, spring creeks, and tailwaters.

Emergence

Yellow Sally nymphs migrate to shore in the long period between April and August. They are important during these migrations and when they gather in gentle edge water waiting to crawl out to emerge. Daily emergence is in late afternoon to evening, at which time trout might key on restless nymphs in the shallows. If your sampling of the stream bottom reveals heavy populations, a Yellow Sally nymph imitation will be effective all day long.

Behavior and Tactics

The Copper John is not an imitation of the Yellow Sally group of nymphs, but a great part of the fly's success might be related to its close resemblance to them. Most, though not all, Yellow Sally nymphs are fairly good swimmers, propelling themselves forward with swift side-to-side undulations of the body. Rig these imitations, perhaps as a pair, with a small yarn or hard indicator, and fish them in the edge shallows. If that fails to move trout, try removing the indicator and fishing them with a swimming retrieve.

Known Hatches

Elk R., BC; Crowsnest R. and Bow R., AB; Yakima R., WA; Willamette R. and McKenzie R., OR; Pit R. and McCleod R., CA; Big Hole R., Madison R., and Yellowstone R., MT; Green R. and Wind R., WY; Green R., UT; North and South Platte, CO.

Yellow Sally adult

Yellow Sally adult

Common names: Yellow Sally, Little Yellow Stone, Yellow Sallfly

Latin names: Perlodidae *Isoperla* (27 Western species); Chloroperlidae *Suwallia* (12) and *Sweltsa* (23)

Size range: #12–16 (7–22 mm, ¼–⅞ inch excluding tails)

Key Features

Tails: Two, usually extend beyond wing tips

Body shape: Elongated, with little taper

Body color: Yellow, tan, to light brown

Wings: Pale yellow to dark brown; in rare species short

Antennae: Long, stout, often dark brown or black

Habitat

Yellow Sallies can be found in streams of almost any size, and at any elevation, throughout the West. They cause selective feeding less on boisterous mountain headwaters than in more placid valley streams and rivers, where they seem to gather in more concentrated numbers, and where trout get better opportunities to focus on them. On some tailwater streams their hatches rival those of Blue-Winged Olive and Pale Morning Dun mayflies.

Emergence

Yellow Sallies often return to the water during egg-laying flights without being noticed. You see them on the surface, and see trout taking them, and it appears to be a midwater hatch, with the adults emerging right up out of the water. It's egg-laying behavior, not an emergence. But they do often drown, and trout take them under the water rather than on top. Carry both a wet fly and a dry fly to fish for them.

Behavior and Tactics

Yellow Sally adults are active in streamside vegetation and are often on the water in scattered numbers throughout the day. But they return in egg-laying flights in late afternoon or evening; earlier on days with heavy cloud cover. Whenever you see them on the water, and notice trout taking them, be sure to ascertain whether the takes are on the surface or beneath it. You can often catch far more trout by swinging a Light Cahill Wet through the rises than you can by drifting a dry fly over them.

Known Hatches

See the listing for nymphs. This is such a widespread hatch, causing selective feeding so often when it happens, that you should always carry the very few flies it takes to be prepared for it. The key is not to overlook it.

Skwala nymph

Skwala nymph

Common name: Skwala

Latin names: Perlodidae *Skwala americana* and *S. curvata*

Size range: #10–12 (16–22 mm, 5/8–7/8 inch excluding tails)

Key Features

Tails: Two, approximately body length, red-brown

Body shape: Long, with little taper; underside with pit in thorax

Body color: Reddish brown; tannish yellow marking on thorax and head

Wing cases: Rear, triangular; front, oval

Gills: Absent from thoracic segments

Antennae: Body length, red-brown

Habitat

Skwala nymphs live in swift riffles and runs. They are distributed across the entire West, but their populations are generally too scattered to cause selective feeding. That changes in a few freestone tailwaters of modest to large size. Though the nymphs live in fast water, they migrate out of it to emerge, and the most common habitat in which you'll fish Skwala imitations is the softer water between riffles and the shoreline.

Emergence

Skwala migrations begin in late February, peak in March and April, and taper off through May and June. Their importance is usually before runoff. Unless you collect them in kick-net samples in riffles, your only clue about their presence will be adults in streamside vegetation and on the water. Anytime you notice even a few dark stoneflies, in between Little Brown Stones and Golden Stones in size, suspect the presence of these nymphs and give an imitation a try.

Skwala Nymph

Behavior and Tactics

Before you tie a specific imitation for Skwala nymphs, be sure they're present in large numbers in the water you plan to fish and that trout have opportunities to feed on them selectively. It's not likely that trout taking an occasional Skwala will let a size 12 Copper John get past them. Whichever nymph you choose, rig to fish it dead-drift on the bottom, either right in riffles or in the calmer water upstream and down, or off to the edges, of the fast water that the naturals must pass through in their migrations to shore.

Known Hatches

Yakima R., WA; Owyhee R., OR; Bow R., AB; Bitterroot R., MT; South Fork Boise R., ID; Gunnison R., CO. Skwala nymphs are so similar in size and color to Golden Stone nymphs that it's certain many more streams have this hatch than are given credit for it.

Skwala adult

Common name: Skwala
Latin names: Perlodidae *Skwala americana* and *S. curvata*
Size range: #10–12 (16–22 mm, 5/8–7/8 inch excluding tails)

Key Features

Tails: Approximately body length
Body shape: Slender; with little taper; pit on underside of thorax
Body color: Golden brown to dark brown
Wings: Female wings normal length; male wings half body length
Antennae: Approximately body length

Habitat

Trout see Skwala adults floating or swimming, rarely more than ten feet from shore. I've seen egg-laden females crawl out of the grass, launch themselves, swim out a few feet, and then drift fifty feet or more until big noses lofted out to intercept them. Even scattered adults on the water will prod pre-runoff trout to take positions in soft edge currents to await the occasional Skwala adult.

Emergence

Though Skwala are most important on cloudy days, that's because most days at that hatch time are overcast. They'll also lay their eggs on sunny days. Activity is greatest during the warmest hours of midafternoon. Because they crawl out of the water before emerging, it's always egg-laying activity you need to notice. It takes a surprisingly small number of Skwala to get trout working. You don't always need an exact imitation, but it will never hurt to have one.

Skwala Egg-Layer

Behavior and Tactics

Because adult Skwala don't fly much, and usually return to the water in sparse numbers, you need to watch carefully for the occasional rise and then target that trout. If you see a single Skwala female on the water, cease casting and follow her float carefully, with binoculars if necessary. When a nose pokes out, get to that spot and cover that area with a dry fly as quickly as you can. Position yourself to achieve the longest possible downstream float. If the trout doesn't respond to a drag-free presentation, try skittering it.

Known Hatches

See the specific listings under Skwala nymphs. But be careful to watch for these midsize stoneflies on any stream or river you fish, especially if you fish early in the season. Skwala adults can provide some surprise dry-fly fishing, with big imitations, over large trout.

Golden Stonefly nymph

Common names: Golden Stone nymph, Willow Fly nymph

Latin names: *Calineuria californica* and *Hesperoperla pacifica* (related *Doroneuria baumanni*, and *Claassenia sabulosa*)

Size range: #4–10 (25–38 mm, 1–1½ inch excluding tails)

Key Features

Tails: Two, approximately body length or longer

Body shape: Stout, with little taper

Body color: *C. cal.*, golden brown, vermiculations on thorax; *H. pac.*, dark brown

Wing cases: Two pairs, prominent

Gills: Tufts at base of each leg; *H. pac.*, tufts between tails

Antennae: Prominent; about body length or shorter

Habitat

Golden Stone nymphs live in tiny headwaters to mature river systems. They are fierce predators and thrive where the bottom consists of rocks with lots of spaces in between where they can prowl and hunt. They are most common in freestone riffles and runs and least common where streambeds are impacted with silt. They live in the fastest water, and are often dislodged, to be fed upon by trout.

Emergence

Golden Stone migrations begin when water temperatures approach 50 degrees F., usually in May and June in the Pacific region, and in June and July in the Rockies. Fish their imitations in the days and weeks prior to the hatch, either in riffles and runs or along the banks. These large nymphs have a two- or three-year life cycle, so they're in the water at all times of year. Use a large imitation during the migration, but a smaller nymph at other times.

Golden Stone Nymph

Behavior and Tactics

Golden Stone nymphs are poor swimmers. When they lose their grip on the bottom, they straighten their bodies and splay their legs, much as a sky diver might. Then they tumble with the current until they regain their grip or get eaten by trout. Rig to get their imitations to the bottom, or very near it, with split shot on the leader, and an indicator 1½ to 2 times the depth of the water up the leader. Fish them dead-drift, either in fast water or along the edges, where the naturals gather for emergence.

Known Hatches

Elk R., BC; Yakima R., WA; N. Pit R. and upper Hat Ck., CA; S. and N. Platte R., Gunnison R., and Colorado R., CO; Green R., UT; Green R., WY; Big Hole R., Madison R., and Yellowstone R., MT; Deschutes R., OR; Bow R., AB.

Golden Stonefly adult

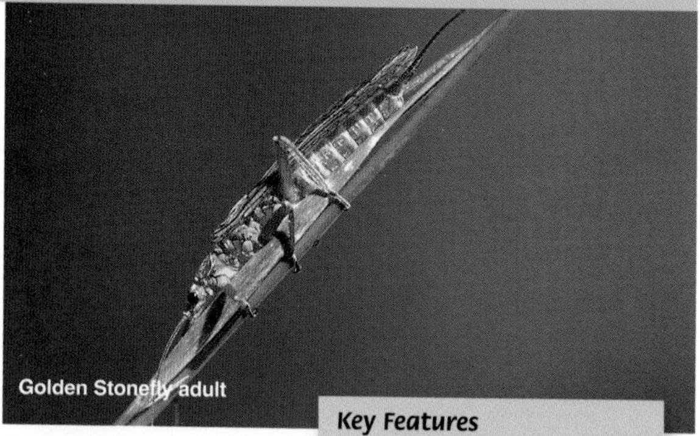
Golden Stonefly adult

Common names: Golden Stone, Willow Fly

Latin names: *Calineuria californica* and *Hesperoperla pacifica* (related *Doroneuria baumanni*, and *Claassenia sabulosa*)

Size range: #4–10 (25–38 mm, 1–1½ inch excluding tails)

Key Features

Tails: Two, stout, body length or shorter

Body shape: Large, stout, with little taper

Body color: Golden to brown on back; yellow to golden brown belly

Wings: Flat over back; gold to brown

Gill remnants: Fleshy knobs at base of each leg

Antennae: Two, prominent

Habitat

Golden Stone adults can be found from the smallest creeks to large rivers with big, broad riffles. You'll also find them on spring creeks and tailwaters, but only where waters with those sources flow though the cobbled riffles and runs that we normally consider to be freestone. Because they're so large, Golden Stone adults can be important even on waters where trout see just a few a day.

Emergence

Golden Stone adults gather along stream edges and crawl around in grass and shrubs. Trout follow the nymph migration and remain at the banks to feed on adults that make mistakes. Occasional midafternoon and evening egg-laying flights can be intense. Fish Golden Stone adult patterns along the edges of fast streams of all sizes. Keep your eye out for females depositing eggs over riffles and runs and for trout feeding on them in midwater currents.

Behavior and Tactics

Golden Stones crawl around, gather to mate, adventure too far out on weak grass stems, or flutter from alder leaves that overhang the water. When they fall in, trout explode on them. Fish their imitations on dead-drift floats right along grassy edges, up underneath alders that shade the water, wherever shrubs crowd the banks. If you notice an egg-laying flight, extend your fishing out over riffles and runs, and be sure to cover any rising trout. On small streams, if you see even two or three Golden Stones in the air, try a Stimulator in all the pools and pockets.

Known Hatches

See the nymph listing for specific hatches. It's more difficult to name Western freestone waters that lack Golden Stones than it is to list those that do. They're everywhere and easily noticed. Be sure to carry imitations of both nymphs and adults.

Salmonfly nymph

Common names: Salmonfly nymph, Giant Salmonfly

Latin name: *Pteronarcys californica* (*P. princeps* and *P. dorsata* not common)

Size range: #2–12 (25–50 mm, 1–2 inches excluding tails)

Key Features

Tails: Two, stout, shorter than body

Body shape: Large, stout, tapered

Body color: Brown to black

Wing cases: Two pairs; prominent

Gills: Tufts on thorax and first two abdominal segments

Antennae: Prominent; approximately body length

Habitat

Salmonfly nymphs are most abundant in large rivers with gradients steep enough to form big and brawling riffles. They browse vegetation growing on rocks in riffles and runs, or consume the detritus that collects under rocks in big, fast water, and are often called the buffalo herds of rivers. They are found in small to medium-sized streams as well, but their most famous hatches are on large Western rivers.

Emergence

Mature Salmonfly nymphs, at their largest sizes, begin migrating toward shore for emergence in late spring and early summer—May and June in coastal regions, June and July in the Rockies. They gather under rocks right at the edges; sometimes a single flat stone two feet from shore will have a dozen or more monstrous nymphs hiding beneath it. Trout follow the migration and then remain at the edges for weeks, feeding on nymphs and then switching to adults.

Behavior and Tactics

During the migration, and when the naturals are gathered along the shoreline, rig with an indicator and shot to fish full-sized Salmonfly nymph imitations dead-drift on the bottom. Fish with upstream casts and downstream drifts in riffles and runs and in the softer water between these and the shoreline. Salmonflies have a three-year life cycle. I tie most of my Salmonfly nymph imitations in smaller sizes, on 10 and 12 hooks, and fish them throughout the year in riffles and runs, usually with a size 16 nymph as a trailer.

Known Hatches

Elk R., BC; Bow R., AB; Yakima R., WA; Deschutes R., OR; Gunnison R., Colorado R., S. and N. Platte R., CO; Provo R., UT; Green R., WY; Henrys and South Fork Snake R., ID; Big Hole R., Madison R., Bitterroot R., Gallatin R., and Beaverhead R., MT.

Salmonfly adult

Common names: Salmonfly, Giant Salmonfly

Latin name: *Pteronarcys californica* (*P. princeps* and *P. dorsata* not common)

Size range: #2–12 (25–50 mm, 1–2 inches excluding tails)

Key Features

Tails: Two, short

Body shape: Large, stout, with little taper

Body color: Back, dark brown to black; belly, often reddish orange

Wings: Held flat over body; heavily veined

Gill remnants: Visible knobs on first two abdominal segments

Antennae: Two, well-developed, body length

Habitat

Salmonfly adults are found most often on big Western rivers. Though associated with freestone rivers, they thrive in a few tailwaters as well, if the water has fast flows and rocky riffles. They're not often important in spring creeks, except in limited freestone sections. Populations are often found in small to medium-sized streams, but they do not often attain enough mass to cause selective feeding.

Emergence

Seasonal emergence begins in May and lasts through June in the Pacific region; it goes from late June through July in the Rockies. Hatches are keyed by water temperatures in the 50-degree F range; you can watch the hatch progress upstream on a single system as the water warms up. Nymphs crawl out at night. The hatch itself is not important. Adults drop to the water constantly. Egg-laying flights do not occur every day but can be massive when they happen.

Behavior and Tactics

Salmonflies, like Golden Stones, hang around in grasses, shrubs, and alders overhanging water. They're awkward climbers and poor fliers. They fall to the water often and have trouble extracting themselves. Trout follow the big nymphs in their migrations to the shorelines of rivers and stay there feeding until the adults cease hanging around a couple of weeks later. Rig to fish these large dry flies on stout 3X tippets. Fish them in edge currents, along grassy banks, and beneath overhanging alder trees and shrubs. Trout will sometimes detonate on them and at other times simply sip them.

Known Hatches

See the nymph section. It's difficult to determine if rivers have famous hatches of Salmonflies or if the same rivers are famous because they have Salmonfly hatches. They're important wherever they're found.

7 Caddisflies

Caddis are sometimes said to be increasing in importance, replacing mayflies as the top trout stream insect in the modern West. It's true in a few places, though far from everywhere. Mayflies still have great hatches on almost all trout waters, and still suffer those twin vulnerabilities to trout of open-water emergence and massed hatches. But it's also true that caddis respond differently to a couple of environmental changes that happen frequently, and that can change the equation for aquatic insects and therefore anglers.

Some caddis groups are able to survive in conditions that cause mayflies to decline, such as pollution, rising water temps that reduce oxygen levels, and silting of stream beds. These things do not necessarily increase the numbers of caddis; caddis simply become more important as these things reduce the numbers of mayflies.

One major change, an increase in the amount of particulate matter in the water, can cause caddis to thrive. Many stream caddis larvae weave miniature gill nets in the current between stones and then feed on drift trapped in the meshes. Water diverted for irrigation and then returned to the main flow entrains lots of tiny particles. Net-spinning caddis populations increase. Plankton doesn't grow in moving water, but a dam on a stream or river creates a stillwater, where plankton forms become abundant. They're delivered downstream in the outflow, and populations of net-spinning caddis can explode. It's a major reason why trout become large in some Western tailwaters: they have more caddis to eat.

Caddis have always been important in terms of numbers eaten by trout, and it's possible that we're just getting around to recognizing that and imitating them when we should.

Caddis adults come in a wide range of sizes and colors, but they're all the same shape: they lack tails, they have short portly bodies, and their wings are tent-shaped, held over their backs, and extend beyond their bodies. Their legs and antennae are usually long, gangly, and prominent.

LIFE CYCLE

Caddis, as opposed to mayflies and stoneflies, have complete metamorphosis, with three life stages: larva, pupa, and adult. The purpose of the transitional pupal stage is to allow greater adaptations in the larval stage, to take advantage of a wider range of habitats. Caddis larvae have no resemblance whatever to the adults that eventually arise from them.

Though we observe caddis adults most often, and are able to see trout feeding on them selectively, trout probably eat more caddis as larvae than either of the other stages. They're likely to feed selectively on pupae more often than they are larvae or adults. It's not

Caddis adult

Caddis pupa

Caddis larva

The caddis life cycle consists of three stages: larva, pupa, and adult. You need to watch closely when caddis are present and trout feed on them, to notice and imitate the stage on which trout are focused.

Free-living larva

Caddis larvae come in three types: free-living, net-spinning, and cased.

Cased larva

Net-spinning larva

easy to notice this subsurface selectivity unless you begin taking screen-net samples, using a throat pump, or killing trout and dissecting them . . . none of which I'm heartily recommending. But I do advise a much greater awareness of what's going on under the water when you see caddis adults in the air.

Most caddis species have a one-year life cycle. A few large ones live two years. In general, they average one to three weeks in the egg, nine to ten months as larvae, two to five weeks as pupae, and two to five weeks as adults. Most are available to trout as larvae; a few are not. Almost all are available as pupae, though a few crawl out on rocks to emerge. Almost all are available as adults in different degrees, depending on their egg-laying behavior. Some avoid trout predation by laying their eggs on leaves overhanging the water, but most lay their eggs on the water's surface and are vulnerable to trout. Many stream caddis dive to the bottom, lay their eggs there, and are taken by trout subsurface rather than floating.

Larval Differences

Caddis larvae are all wormlike or grublike, but they exist in three forms: free-living, net-spinning, and cased. Free-living types build no case, are predaceous, and do not often cause selective feeding because their populations are evenly distributed, not concentrated, and not frequently found abundant in the drift. Net-spinners can be dense on streams with irrigation return or tailwater flows. When they get crowded, they disperse by letting go and entering the drift. Trout often focus on them. Cased caddis are vulnerable when they leave the old case behind, drift freely on the current in large numbers, and return to the bottom to build a new case. Some vegetation-cased types are fed on selectively, case and all, but more often in lakes and ponds than in creeks, streams, and rivers.

Whenever you encounter caddis, observe carefully to see which stage trout are focused and feeding upon. It's most common to match the adults you see in the air and on the water, but the same adults can sometimes be your indication to fish a larval imitation, a pupal pattern, or even a wet fly matching the diving adult.

Spotted Sedge larva

Common names: Net-Spinner, Spotted Sedge larva, Green Rock Worm

Latin name: *Hydropsyche* (approximately 25 Western species)

Size range: #10–16 (12–18 mm, ½–¾ inch)

Key Features

Anal hooks: Large, with tuft of hairs at base of each

Abdomen: Thickly branched gills on underside

Abdomen color: Dirty tan to olive to bright green

Thorax: Hardened shield on back of each segment

Thorax color: Amber to brown; shields with patterning

Habitat

Net-spinning caddis larvae thrive in rocky riffles and runs but also live on flats and in glides as long as the current is steady. Though they prefer rocky bottoms, they're also found anchored on woody debris. Because of their need for particulate drift, they're most common in freestone flows with leaf debris, in tailwaters that supply plankton, or in return flows after a stream has been diverted for irrigation.

Emergence

Spotted Sedge larvae are most important when they reach their mature sizes and greatest densities in the weeks and even months before they seal themselves in the pupal cocoon prior to emergence. With this widespread and diverse group, that will be any time between March in the lowland regions and September at higher altitudes. If you hoist stones from a streambed and observe net-spinning caddis larvae, you'll know trout are seeing a lot more of them than you are.

Behavior and Tactics

Grublike net-spinning larvae caught in the drift, whether knocked loose by the current or disbursing in the drift to get away from too many neighbors, have no ability to swim. They curl at least slightly and then let the water deliver them where it will. If they avoid trout and get back to the bottom, they proceed to build a new net and retreat. Rig to fish their imitations dead-drift, just above the bottom, on a shot-and-indicator setup.

Known Hatches

Famous places to fish net-spinning caddis larvae would be a list of famous trout streams and rivers throughout the West. But this group is also important on waters that are not famous. Never be without imitations for them. You'll use them wherever you fish for trout.

Spotted Sedge pupa

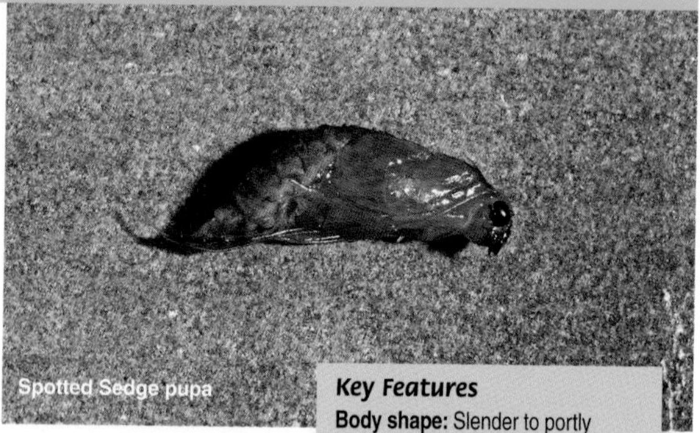

Common name: Spotted Sedge pupa

Latin name: *Hydropsyche* (approximately 25 Western species)

Size range: #10–16 (12–18 mm, ½–¾ inch)

Key Features

Body shape: Slender to portly

Body color: Yellowish tan to olive to bright green

Wing cases: Brown to olive; darker than body

Gills: Tufts on abdominal segments

Note: Caddis pupae are difficult to identify at any level without a microscope and keys. Often the best way to recognize them is by associating them with the appropriate larvae or adults.

Habitat

Spotted sedge pupae arise from the same riffles and runs inhabited by their larvae. Pupation takes place in the larval retreat. You can collect the pupae by lifting rocks out of the current, looking for shelters made of pebbles and bits of leaves and bark, and extracting the pupal cocoons from them. You can also associate the pupae with swarms of spotted sedge adults at streamside, almost always in the evening.

Emergence

With twenty-five Western species, emergence of spotted sedges is spread from May to October on different waters. Numbers are usually heavy for each hatch, so you'll have no trouble noticing the adults during their two- to three-week dominant period. Associated pupae will leave their cocoons at evening, rise quickly through the water column, suspend for a moment beneath the surface, and then emerge through it. The hatch often continues after dark.

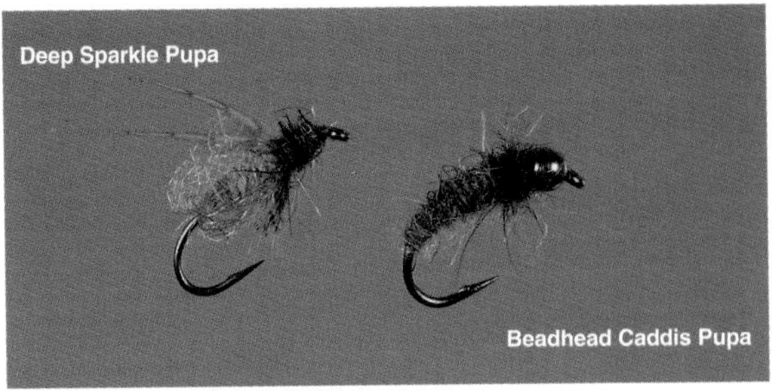

Behavior and Tactics

Spotted Sedge pupae stage along the bottom, drift for a few feet, and then swim to the top, where they drift again. This indicates three possible methods. Rig to fish the Deep Sparkle Pupa with indicator and shot, dead-drift along the bottom. Drift or swim either pupa pattern in the mid-depths, a foot or so down, on a wet-fly swing. Rig to fish the Beadhead Caddis Pupa shallow and dead-drift, up until dark. It's effective to suspend either pupa pattern under a small indicator or behind an imitation of the Spotted Sedge adult.

Known Hatches

Elk R., BC; Bow R., AB; Yakima R., WA; Deschutes R., OR; Hat Ck., CA; San Juan R., NM; Colorado R., AZ; S. and N. Platte R., CO; Provo R., UT; Green R., WY; Madison R. and Missouri R., MT.

Spotted Sedge adult

Spotted Sedge adult

Common names: Spotted Sedge, Cinnamon Sedge
Latin name: *Hydropsyche* (approximately 25 Western species)
Size range: #10–16 (12–18 mm, ½–¾ inch)

Key Features

Body color: Tan to dark green
Wings: Brown, spotted with gray
Legs: Front legs with well-developed spurs
Antennae: Body length

Note: As with caddis pupae, adult caddis are difficult to separate accurately without a microscope and keys. It's easy to choose an effective pattern based on size, shape, and color.

Habitat

Spotted Sedges are most abundant in tailwaters, where plankton drifts into their feeding nets. This group is least important in headwater streams, and most important in more mature stream and river systems. Their numbers will be replaced by the related Little Sister Sedges, covered in the next section, as you move farther down watersheds toward the beginnings of warm-water dominance.

Emergence

Adult caddis live for a few days to one or two weeks. Their numbers accumulate, and trout see them in greater abundance, as a hatch continues. They mate in vegetation along stream and river banks. You'll often see flights of Spotted Sedges madly circling sage and juniper tops in the setting sun. These indicate fishing a pupa pattern as prescribed in the preceding pages, one of the adult dressings given below, or a combination of the two.

Behavior and Tactics

Spotted Sedge females lay their eggs on the bottom. They fly down to strike the surface, penetrate through it, and then swim frantically. Always try imitating the adults with either the listed emerger or the high-floating Elk Hair Caddis adult. Most of the time, one of the two will work. If you encounter refusals, however, revert to a pupal pattern or swing a traditional winged wet fly. They're not shown here for space reasons, but the March Brown Spider soft-hackle and standard Hare's Ear wet fly might solve those evening situations when trout feed on diving adults.

Known Hatches

Again, to list the known hatches of the Spotted Sedge would be to list almost all flowing Western waters. They're most important where they're most abundant; you might find them in great numbers on any water you fish. It's imperative to carry imitations at all times.

Little Sister Sedge larva

Common names: Little Sister Sedge larva, Little Green Rock Worm

Latin name: Cheumatopsyche (approximately 15 Western species)

Size range: #14–18 (7–10 mm, 1⁄4–7⁄16 inch)

Key Features

Anal hooks: Large, with tuft of hairs at base of each

Abdomen: Thickly branched gills on underside

Abdomen color: Pale to dark olive

Thorax: Hardened shield on back of each segment

Thorax color: Amber to brown; shields lack patterning

Habitat

Little Sister Sedges are siblings to the larger Spotted Sedges. They're similar as larvae, slightly smaller, and often pale green. Just as often, you can't separate them without a microscope and can use the same patterns to imitate them, tied a size or two smaller. They spin nets with slightly smaller mesh sizes and are adapted to filtering more refined particles from currents farther downstream in large river systems.

Emergence

The importance of Little Sister Sedge larvae ends when they seal themselves in their retreats for the pupal stage. Hatches tend toward middle to late summer; larval peaks are in spring and early summer, when the most larvae are out and in the drift most often. If you hoist rocks from riverbeds during that period, and find small, wormlike larvae in pale to dark olive, imitate them with a Pale Caddis Larva or with the smallest larval imitations for Spotted Sedges.

Pale Caddis Larva

Behavior and Tactics

When cast loose in the currents, Little Sister Sedge larvae tumble on the drift until they return to the bottom or get eaten by trout. Rig to fish their imitations dead-drift on the bottom. Because they live most commonly in big rivers, you'll almost always have to get them three to five feet down. That will require split shot or putty weight on the leader near the nymph, and a strike indicator at the opposite end. Because they are small patterns, it's often helpful to rig them as point flies, in tandem with a heavier nymph.

Known Hatches

Yakima R., WA; Willamette and Deschutes R., OR; Bow R., AB; Big Hole R. and Missouri R., MT. These are a few of the places I've fished over Little Sister Sedges myself or have reliable reports from others who have. Little Sister Sedge larvae are widespread and are probably reported most often as Spotted Sedge larvae.

Little Sister Sedge pupa

Common name: Little Sister Sedge pupa
Latin name: *Cheumatopsyche* (approximately 15 Western species)
Size range: #14–20 (5–10 mm, 3⁄16–7⁄16 inch)

Key Features

Body color: Pale olive to green
Wing cases: Olive to light brown; darker than body
Gills: Tufts on abdominal segments

Habitat

Little Sister Sedge pupae generally escape from the larval retreat in broader and calmer currents, on larger rivers, than the bigger Spotted Sedges. I've fished them most often over wide, flat reaches of rivers that flow over freestone bottoms covered with baseball- to softball-sized stones. But they're not restricted to such big waters; they're also abundant on smaller pastoral streams where irrigation return is a factor.

Emergence

Seasonal emergence peaks in July and August in most places. Daily hatches tend toward the cool morning and evening hours. They're typically absent during the midday heat. It's possible that the greatest abundance of them hatch after dark or before daylight. Like Spotted Sedge pupae, they emerge from the cocoon, stage briefly along the bottom, swim quickly toward the top, and stage briefly again just subsurface before emerging through it.

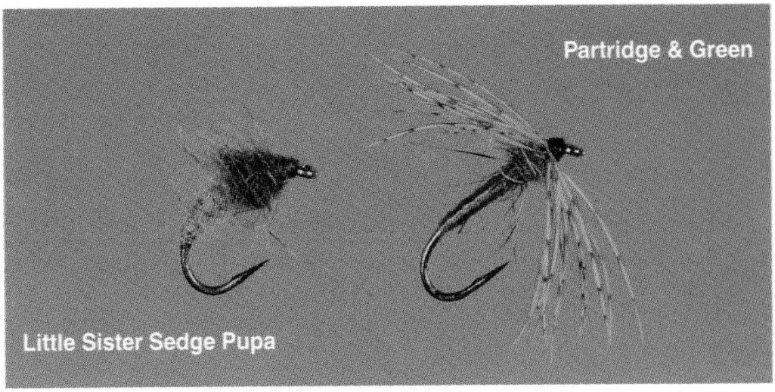

Behavior and Tactics

If the river you're fishing has Little Sister Sedges, it's beneficial to rig a pupa pattern to fish the bottom during pre-hatch periods. Use it as the small nymph in a two-nymph tandem. Fish it dead-drift just above the bottom. I prefer to fish a pupal pattern during a mid-morning hatch, when I notice trout working. Then I rig it as a wet fly and fish it inches deep on a very gentle, slow swing, through working trout. A pupa can also be dropped off a dry imitation or beneath a yarn indicator.

Known Hatches

Look for Little Sister Sedge hatches in the downstream regions of all major Western river systems and on any pastoral stream to which you have access. Some big rivers, like the Deschutes, have heavy hatches of these that are usually mistaken for Spotted Sedges.

Little Sister Sedge adult

Little Sister Sedge adult

Common name: Little Sister Sedge

Latin name: *Cheumatopsyche* (approximately 15 Western species)

Size range: #14–20 (5–10 mm, 3⁄16–7⁄16 inch)

Key Features

Body color: Pale olive to dark green

Wings: Light to dark brown, mottled

Legs: Front legs with well-developed spurs

Antennae: Body length

Habitat

These are reduced Spotted Sedges, though I've fished over them more often in very pale colors than the darker colors of the larger caddis, so I tie a separate set of imitations for the adults and pupae. Because the larvae live in the downstream ends of river systems, and in gentle pastoral streams, adult imitations are fished more often on smooth water than rough.

Emergence

Seasonal emergence starts in June, peaks in July and August, and tapers off in early September. Daily emergence in my own experience tends to be in the cool hours of morning, on hot days, beginning around 7 a.m. and lasting until 10 or 11 a.m. The adults pop through the surface film; many of them hop and skitter a bit before getting airborne. A collecting net suspended in the surface currents will reveal many cripples, unable to escape the pupal shuck.

Behavior and Tactics

The natural insect is usually taken by trout while placidly riding smooth currents. The olive X-Caddis has no hackle, lowering the body flush into the surface film, and with its trailing shuck represents cripples. It's excellent for smooth water. I recommend either clipping the hackle from the underside of the Elk Hair-style dry or using it to suspend a pupa pattern on about twenty inches of fine tippet. Fish both on dead-drift floats, usually from a cross-stream or upstream position. You don't want to line trout sipping these tiny caddis on smooth water.

Known Hatches

There are few known hatches of Little Sister Sedges, but it's likely that a fair number of hatches thought to be Spotted Sedges are actually their smaller siblings.

Gray Sedge adult

Gray Sedge adult

Common names: Gray Sedge, Green Sedge
Latin name: *Rhyacophila* (approximately 90 Western species)
Size range: #10–14 (8–16 mm, ¼–¾ inch)

Key Features

Body color: Dark green
Wings: Dark gray, often speckled with light dots
Antennae: Slightly shorter than body

Habitat

Free-living Gray Sedge larvae, known as Green Rock Worms, are predaceous, and therefore dispersed. In my experience, trout don't feed selectively on either larval or pupal stages. They do focus at times on the adults. The larvae prowl the spaces between stones in the fastest riffles, runs, and even cascades. You'll find trout feeding on their adults as they deposit eggs over the same freestone riffles, often out in the middle of big water.

Emergence

Hatches are spread from spring through fall, in one or another of the ninety species. Daily hatch periods are as scattered as the number of species. But you want to fish the egg-laying flights, not the hatch. You'll see dark gray caddis adults over the water and splashy rises in their midst. I've always done well with the Deer Hair Caddis dry fly. Females swim down to lay their eggs, so if the dry fails, try swinging the Leadwing Coachman wet fly.

Behavior and Tactics

Gray Sedge adults bounce above the water over boisterous riffles on mountain streams at midday, in bright sunshine. Their behavior seems frivolous, but they're about the business of laying their eggs. Though it's likely more of them are taken by trout beneath the surface, as they swim down to lay their eggs, it's more fun to fish a high-floating dry and coax those splashy rises. If the dry fly fails though, or it's too difficult to keep it afloat on the rough water, switch to fishing the wet fly on the swing.

Known Hatches

Very few freestone creeks, streams, and rivers lack the Gray Sedge. You will not find trout selective on all of them, but when you do, you should be armed with the pair of standard patterns it takes to match them.

Little Black Short-Horned Sedge larva

Little Black Short-Horned Sedge larva

Common names: Little Tan Short-Horned Sedge larva, Turtle-Case Maker, *Glossosoma*

Latin name: *Glossosoma* (approximately 20 Western species)

Size range: #16–20 (5–8 mm, $\frac{3}{16}$–$\frac{5}{16}$ inch)

Key Features

Case: Domed, turtlelike; made of pebbles

Anal hooks: Small; lack tufts of hairs

Gills: Tufts of filaments absent

Body shape: Short, compact; maggotlike

Body color: White to pale tan; brown or black head

Thorax: Single hardened plate

Habitat

These larvae have adapted to nearly all stream habitats. They're found in waters of all sizes and at all elevations. They're most common in moderate to fast currents, because that type of water has the most rocky bottom structure. They won't be found on silted bottoms. They're equally at home in spring creeks, tailwaters, and freestone streams, so long as the bottom is rocky and the stones clean.

Emergence

The maggotlike larvae of the turtle-case makers outgrow and leave their old cases frequently during their one-year life cycle, and because of their great numbers, they are common components of biotic drift. They'll be most abundant, and most often seen by trout, in spring and early summer. Trout see enough of them on a daily basis to be aware of the delicacy of a natural. An imitation makes an effective trailer fly in any two-nymph combination.

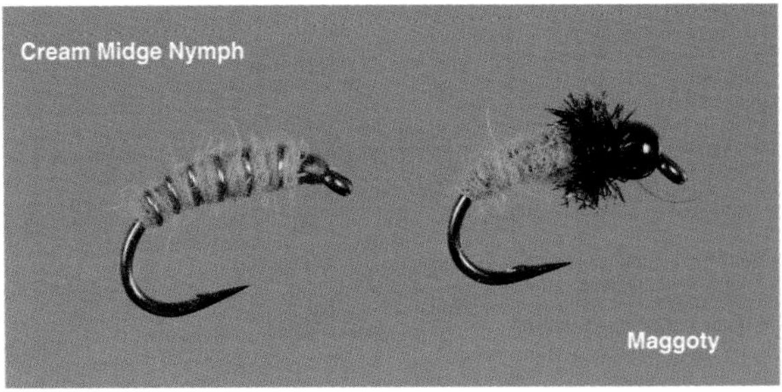

Behavior and Tactics

Like all caddis larvae, these are helpless when loose in the drift. Because of the natural density of that compact body, they remain near the bottom. Rig to get the fly as close to the stones as you can. In shallow water that is not swift, you might be able to do that with a single weighted imitation and a yarn indicator two to five feet above it. In most cases, you'll need to add split shot, putty weight, or a larger and more heavily-weighted nymph. However you rig, present the fly dead-drift without any unnatural movement.

Known Hatches

These are less a famous hatch phenomena than they are the type of insect that can be found on almost all moving waters, catching the attention of trout almost everywhere in the West you might fish. You should always carry a few tiny patterns to match them.

Little Black Short-Horned Sedge pupa

Little Black Short-Horned Sedge pupa

Common names: Little Tan Short-Horned Sedge Pupa, Turtle-Case Maker, *Glossosoma*

Latin name: *Glossosoma* (approximately 20 Western species)

Size range: #16–20 (5–8 mm, 3⁄16–5⁄16 inch)

Key Features

Body shape: Compact; maggotlike

Body color: White to pale tan or pale olive

Gills: Absent

Wing cases: Brown to almost black

Habitat

Turtle-case larvae migrate out of fast water and form colonies in moderate currents for pupation. Pupae are important in edge currents alongside swift riffles and runs or upstream and down from them. They can also be important on freestone flats with even flows over clean stones. Your clue to the importance of these small pupae is the presence of myriads of small, dark caddis adults trotting busily in streamside grasses and shrubs.

Emergence

These small caddis are most important at times when larger insects do not distract trout. Though they peak in April, May, and June, then again in September and October, I've fished over them as early as February and as late as November. Daily emergence is difficult to pin down, though it's generally in the evening. It's a good rule to swing or dead-drift a pupal pattern any time you see adults but get no takes to floating imitations.

Behavior and Tactics

Short-Horned Sedge pupae are very active swimmers, though if they're caught in swift currents they have little control over their ascent to the surface. Try fishing their imitations in one of two ways. First, suspend them beneath a yarn indicator or a dry fly on a two- to three-foot tippet, and fish them on upstream casts, with dead-drift presentations. If that fails, try dispensing with the indicator or dry, rigging the pupa pattern as a wet fly, or preferably as one of a pair of them, and fishing them on a slow swing.

Known Hatches

Elk R., BC; Yakima R., WA; Deschutes R., OR; McCleod R. and Sacramento R., CA; Bow R., AB; Big Hole R. and Madison R., MT; Green R. and Wind R., WY; Green R., UT; Frying Pan R., CO; Rio Grande R., NM; Colorado R., AZ.

Little Black Short-Horned Sedge adult

Little Black Short-Horned Sedge adult

Common names: Little Black Short-Horned Sedge, *Glossosoma*
Latin name: *Glossosoma* (approximately 20 Western species)
Size range: #16–20 (5–10 mm, 3⁄16–3⁄8 inch)

Key Features

Body color: Tan to dark green
Wings: Light to dark brown, often mottled
Antennae: Body length or shorter

Habitat

Glossosoma adults hatch in softer edge currents to the sides of main flows that are often brutal. I fish them most often on benches and boulder-garden flats on the insides of heavy riffles and runs. I've also fished them on freestone flats. I see them more often in streamside grasses than on the water; their presence alongside the stream is an indication that an imitation will work.

Emergence

Seasonal emergence peaks on different rivers at a wide variety of times but will usually be sometime between April and June on low-land streams and between July and October at higher altitudes. Always be on the watch for the small and busy adults in streamside vegetation. If you see them, trout will be feeding on them, though you'll rarely observe it happening. Daily importance is usually in late afternoon and evening, often in the last half hour before dark.

Behavior and Tactics

Adults of the Little Short-Horned Sedge are as active on the water as they are in the grasses alongside the river. Try fishing your floating imitation dead drift, but if that fails, give it an occasional scoot or twitch, then let it rest. The Deer Hair Caddis is excellent because it allows this movement. If a dry fly fails, try suspending a Starling & Herl soft hackle behind a yarn indicator or dry fly. You might also fish a pair of small wets on a slow swing in edge currents where you notice trout working on *Glossosoma* adults.

Known Hatches

See the pupal listing. Because they are ubiquitous in the West, you should always carry the full range of larva, pupa, and adult patterns for the Little Short-Horned Sedges. Even if you don't use them to match a hatch, they all make wonderful small searching patterns.

American Grannom larva

Common names: Mother's Day Caddis larva, American Grannom, Black Caddis

Latin names: *Brachycentrus occidentalis* and *B. americanus*

Size range: #12–16 (10–17 mm, ⅜–⅝ inch)

Key Features

Case: Usually square in cross-section; made of vegetation

Anal hooks: Modest size; tufts of hairs at base

Body shape: Long; somewhat stout

Body color: Off-white to green

Thorax: Hardened plates on first two segments

Habitat

Grannom larvae inhabit all but the swiftest currents. They can be found on rocky bottoms and in rooted vegetation and are often prolific in weedy edge currents and backwaters. They colonize, gathering on one rock while the bottom around it is almost empty of them. The case is extended as they grow, rather than replaced, so they are not often found in the drift as uncased larvae.

Emergence

The larvae fasten their cases to rocks, seal themselves inside, and pupate in safety from trout. Once this preparation for emergence begins, the importance of the larval stage ends. Mother's Day Caddis pupate in early to late spring; Black Caddis, in late summer and fall. But their emergences are so prolonged that you'll find larvae being taken by trout through most of the fishing season on one water or another. Trout feed on them case and all.

Behavior and Tactics

Like almost all caddis larvae, cased or uncased, Grannoms are unable to swim. When knocked loose in the currents, they become twigs on the drift. The bead on the second listed imitation is based on my theory that the wink of light it gives off signals life to a trout and hopefully separates the fly from other bits of drift that fail to look alive. I don't know if the theory works, but I do know the imitation does. Both should be rigged to fish near the bottom and presented dead-drift.

Known Hatches

See entry for adults, for which the hatch is best known. These larval dressings make good searching patterns on all streams and rivers that have populations of cased caddis, which is all Western waters.

American Grannom pupa

American Grannom pupa (Jim Schollmeyer)

Common names: Mother's Day Caddis pupa, American Grannom, Black Caddis
Latin names: *Brachycentrus occidentalis* and *B. americanus*
Size range: #14–18 (8–15 mm, 5⁄16–5⁄8 inch)

Key Features

Body color: Pale olive to green, with brown stripe on back
Wing cases: Light to dark brown or black
Gills: Tufts absent

Habitat

Though their larvae are found on streams of all sizes, I've had my best fishing over Grannom hatches with pupal patterns on gentle tailwater flows or on the broad and less than boisterous reaches of mature Western rivers. Prime examples are the gentle Bighorn River tailwater in south-central Montana and the broad flows of the Yellowstone River in Paradise Valley, though I've enjoyed them in many other places.

Emergence

American Grannoms can be split into two major hatches: early spring Mother's Day Caddis (*B. occidentalis*) and late summer and fall Black Caddis (*B. americanus*). The first emerges just before runoff on such rivers as the Madison and Yellowstone; the latter, on the Bighorn and many other rivers as summer fades into fall. Daily emergences of the early hatch are in the warmest hours of afternoon. The later hatch tends to come off from late morning to early afternoon.

Behavior and Tactics

Mother's Day Caddis hatch in great numbers over a fairly short time, an hour or two. You'll see noses poking out to feed greedily on them. You'll manage to surprise some of those noses with dry flies, if you stick to fishing them. But a pupa pattern fished on the swing just subsurface will often fool more of them. Late summer and fall Black Caddis hatches are on smoother water, over more demanding trout. If a dry fly fails to fool trout, try fishing a pupa pattern on a very slow swing through a pod of rising trout.

Known Hatches

Pupal patterns for the Mother's Day Caddis and Black Caddis are most important where hatches are fairly heavy and trout somewhat difficult. Where hatches are less intense, and trout less often pestered by anglers, you can usually do as well or better with a floating imitation.

American Grannom adult

American Grannom adult

Common names: Mother's Day Caddis, American Grannom, Black Caddis
Latin names: *Brachycentrus occidentalis* and *B. americanus*
Size range: #14–18 (8–15 mm, 5⁄16–5⁄8 inch)

Key Features

Body color: Pale olive to dark green, often with brown stripe on back
Wings: Dark gray, brown, to almost black
Antennae: Body length or shorter

Habitat

Grannoms almost always emerge on peaceful reaches of medium streams to large rivers. Emergence is in association with the shoreline, though not often right on it. The small adults form drift lines five to ten feet wide, about the same distance off the banks. On wide flats they might form a band fifteen to twenty feet wide, drifting downstream twenty to forty feet from the bank.

Emergence

The Mother's Day Caddis hatches in the first weeks of May in the warmest hours of the afternoon. If you're lucky, the hatch will start before runoff. The late summer and fall hatch of Black Caddis often begins before noon and lasts two or three hours. Return flights for egg-laying can continue from late afternoon until dark, so the hatch seems to go on for hours, and trout feed as long as adults are on the water.

Behavior and Tactics

Because the naturals sit on the water without much commotion, present their imitations with dead-drift floats. You'll usually be working fairly flat currents, over trout that have seen lots of flies pass over their heads. You can often get away with upstream casts in the early Mother's Day Caddis hatch, but you will almost always be forced to use cross-stream reach casts or downstream wiggle casts to fool trout during the later Black Caddis hatch. Three- to four-foot tippets of 5X or even 6X are sometimes needed to fool sophisticated trout during this hatch.

Known Hatches

Mother's Day Caddis: Yellowstone R. and Madison R., MT; Yakima R., WA; Willamette and Deschutes R., OR; N. Platte R., CO. Black Caddis: Bighorn R., MT; Crooked R., OR. This short list is restricted to hatches I've fished or had reliable reports about. There are many, many others.

Little Western Weedy-Water Sedge pupa

Little Western Weedy-Water Sedge pupa
(Jim Schollmeyer)

Common names: Little Western Weedy-Water Sedge pupa, Little Grannom
Latin name: *Amiocentrus aspilus*
Size range: #16–22 (8–10 mm, 5⁄16–5⁄8 inch)

Key Features

Body shape: Somewhat slender, elongated
Body color: Pale olive to green
Wing cases: Dark brown
Gills: Tufts absent

Habitat

Amiocentrus larvae make vegetation cases that are slender and cylindrical. They prefer slow currents in medium to large rivers and are most prevalent where vegetation takes root. The larvae are not important as models for imitation. They pupate in the larval case, and their pupae become important as they swim toward the surface along the edges of rather tame flows.

Emergence

Weedy-Water Sedge hatches begin in March and last until September and October. I have fished them in spring on Oregon's Crooked River and then again in September on Montana's Bighorn. Daily emergence is in midafternoon for the early and late seasonal hatches and in the evening during midsummer warm weather.

Because the larvae live in weedy edge currents, you'll fish over the pupae within a few feet of shore, unless rooted plants extend outward into slow center currents.

Behavior and Tactics

These pupae leave the larval case in slow water and make their way to the top through a likely gauntlet of feeding trout. Try rigging your pupa pattern, or a brace of them, on a three- to four-foot dropper tippet off a yarn indicator, and use a dead-drift presentation. If that fails to fool fish, remove the indicator and move into position to fish the imitations on a slow to medium swing. Give them time to sink, and then animate them, swimming and lifting them at the same time. That might move the trout.

Known Hatches

Yakima R., WA; Metolius and Crooked R., OR; Hat Ck., CA; Bighorn and Missouri R., MT; Henrys and South Fork Snake R., ID; Green R., UT. A common thread runs through these streams: most are large, and most are spring creeks or tamed by dams.

Little Western Weedy-Water Sedge adult

Little Western Weedy-Water Sedge adult

Key Features

Body color: Light to dark green, often with tan or olive stripes on sides

Wings: Dark grayish brown; heavily veined

Antennae: Body length or shorter

Common names: Little Western Weedy-Water Sedge, Little Grannom

Latin name: *Amiocentrus aspilus*

Size range: #16–22 (8–10 mm, 5⁄16–5⁄8 inch)

Habitat

Because they emerge from larvae that inhabit slow and usually vegetated habitat, Little Weedy-Water Sedge adults hatch on slow currents, usually on rivers of medium size and larger. They are found far more often on spring creek and tailwater flats than they are in freestone streams. You will almost invariably imitate the adults in association with the shoreline or rooted vegetation beds on water that is at least somewhat smooth.

Emergence

If the weather is at all warm, during their summer hatches, the winged Weedy-Water Sedge adult escapes the surface quickly, with just a two- to five-foot float. In cooler weather, during their fall hatches, the adults are often on the water for five to ten feet, sometimes more. In my experience over them, most of it on the Bighorn River in September, trout set up in pods to sip on the helpless adults, working them patiently.

Behavior and Tactics

Though they've been reported to hop fitfully on the water before lifting off to escape it, I've observed Little Weedy-Water Sedge adults drifting placidly in all of my own fishing. You might try a bit of skittering if a dead-drift presentation fails, but I've found a float without movement is most useful during the hatch. The type of water where these little caddis hatch attracts heavy fishing pressure. It's critical to extend your leader with three to four feet of 5X or 6X tippet and to position yourself for cross-stream reach casts or downstream wiggle casts.

Known Hatches

Little Weedy-Water Sedges are scarce or absent at the northern and southern ranges of caddis distribution: Alberta, British Columbia, Arizona, New Mexico, and Nevada. They're most abundant across the central tier of states, from the Pacific Coast to the Rockies.

Long-Horned Sedge adult

Long-Horned Sedge adult

Common names: Tan Spotted-Wing Long-Horned Sedge, *Oecetis*
Latin name: *Oecetis avara* (5 related Western species)
Size range: #14–18 (11–12 mm, ⅝–½ inch)

Key Features
Body color: Yellow-olive to tan or brown
Wings: Light tan to brown; some with dark dots; long and slender
Antennae: Much longer than body

Habitat

Oecetis live in fairly placid waters; some are also present in stillwaters. The dominant species, *O. avara*, is best known for a single hatch on the Missouri River tailwater in Montana, where it's abundant and important. The larvae are cased, bottom dwellers, and predaceous. They prefer quiet current areas, so their consequent adults emerge right along the edges. Neither the larvae nor the pupae have been reported to cause selective feeding.

Emergence

The most famous Missouri River hatch has a mid-July peak, with a two- to three-week emergence period. Daily hatches are in afternoon and evening. I've fished them in the weed-filled shoreline waters of the Missouri near Craig in July and August, almost always as light begins to fail. They're usually mixed with Spotted Sedges that are roughly the same size, though a bit darker in color. The hatch is fairly widespread but hasn't been recorded as important anywhere else.

Behavior and Tactics

These small caddis adults drift quietly along the edges of the big Missouri River or get caught in its lazy eddies. Trout set up stations and sip them daintily. Hooking the trout becomes a matter of getting your imitation in front of the fish at the moment it's ready to rise again. Presentation is just as important as accurately matching the hatch. The listed dressings separate your offerings from the average Elk Hair Caddis the trout see on the heavily-fished river. Refine your gear and your tactics as much as you do the fly pattern you select.

Known Hatches

Beyond that famous hatch on the Missouri River, this ginger Long-Horned Sedge is relatively obscure. A taxonomic species list of collection records shows it, or one of its near relatives, present in every Western state and province outside of New Mexico and Nevada.

Fall Caddis larva

Common names: Fall Caddis, October Caddis
Latin name: *Dicosmoecus* (4 related Western species)
Size range: #6–12 (25–40 mm, 1–1½ inch)

Key Features

Case: Large, made of pebbles
Anal hooks: Small; lacking tufts of hairs
Body: Large and portly; white to yellow
Gills: Profuse branched gills
Thorax: Hardened plates on first two segments

Habitat

These large larvae prefer rocky bottoms. Beyond that their restrictions are few: They are found in Western streams of all sizes, at all elevations. They can be found in placid edge waters and also in fairly swift riffles. They are most abundant in freestone streams and rivers but are also present in spring creeks and tailwaters. They crawl on the faces of rocks, feeding on diatoms and algae that grow there.

Emergence

Fall Caddis emerge in September and October, but the importance of their larvae peaks in mid to late summer, before they enter pupation. Though I've not observed it personally, the larvae are reported to leave their cases and enter the drift, with at least a few on the currents every late afternoon. It's hard to imagine a trout having trouble deciding what to do about such a large and bright chunk of nutrition drifting into its gunsights.

Fall Caddis Larva

Behavior and Tactics

Because of their size and density, these larvae are more likely to tumble along near the bottom than to ride higher in the water column. You'll need split shot or putty weight on the leader to get an imitation down. It will take a substantial indicator to float that weight. I've come to prefer the large-size balloon indicators. In a two-nymph tandem, a Fall Caddis Larva makes a good upper fly. Trail it with a size 16 or so generic pattern. You'll hook the most fish on the small fly, but the larger one might attract them to it.

Known Hatches

Very few streams in the West lack Fall Caddis larvae, though they're not important in all of them. Assess their numbers by observing bottom rocks along the edges of fast water. If you see lots of these clumsy cased caddis crawling about, try an imitation.

Fall Caddis pupa

Common names: Fall Caddis, October Caddis
Latin name: *Dicosmoecus* (4 related Western species)
Size range: #6–12 (20–25 mm, ¾–1 inch)

Key Features

Body: Brown stripe on back; black fringe on abdomen
Color: White or yellow; amber when mature
Wing cases: Dark gray or brown when mature
Gills: Visible branched gills on sides of abdomen

Habitat

Fall Caddis larvae migrate close to shore and fasten their cases to the undersides of stones. Pupation takes three to five weeks. When mature, pupae cut their way out of the cases, swim the remaining short distance to shore, and crawl out on protruding rocks to emerge. You'll see their abandoned shucks on stones in the shallows. They'll favor short stretches of shoreline and certain rocks.

Emergence

Fall Caddis hatch in September and October, in some places trailing into November. Daily emergence is in late afternoon, early evening, or after dark. The importance of pupal patterns is controversial. On many waters they crawl out in such shallow water, so close to shore, that trout can't get at them. On many others, however, a pupal pattern dead-drifted in any edge flows where the naturals are present will con selective trout. If you notice naturals, try them.

Brick Back Caddis

Behavior and Tactics

These big pupae are agile swimmers. If the setup is right, you might be able to cast from the bank, and let the pupa pattern swing in to the edge downstream from you. If trout are holding tight to the same bank, you might coax them into thumping the fly when it's fished almost like a streamer. However, the edges are rarely shaped correctly for such fishing, and you're usually better off rigging the nymph beneath an indicator, with or without weight on the leader, and fishing it dead-drift, with upstream casts, in the currents just off shore.

Known Hatches

Elk R., BC; Red Deer R., AB; Upper Columbia R., WA; Deschutes R., OR; Sacramento R. and McCleod R., CA; Missouri R. and Big Hole R., MT; Wind R. and Green R., WY; Green R. and Provo R., UT; Colorado R. and Gunnison R., CO; Rio Grande R., NM.

Fall Caddis adult

Fall Caddis adult

Common names: Fall Caddis, October Caddis
Latin name: *Dicosmoecus* (4 related Western species)
Size range: #6–12 (20–30 mm, ¾–1¼ inch)

Key Features
Body: Large, orange to amber
Wings: Dark gray, with distinct black veins
Antennae: Approximately body length

Habitat

Some Fall Caddis adults deposit their eggs by attaching them to alder and other leaves overhanging the water. I've watched adults bouncing on edge currents to shed egg masses, but I've not seen trout take one. Other anglers report the adults taken greedily by trout. They're large bites, and you should carry an imitation and fish it up under trees and along the edges.

Emergence

Hatches are heaviest in September and October. Fish the pupa pattern during the emergence and an adult imitation when you see them on the water, usually in afternoon and evening. The naturals are excellent flyers and spend time batting around shrubs, grasses, and trees along the shoreline. Fish their imitations from a foot to five feet out from the banks. If the adult inspires no takes, try dropping a pupal pattern off its stern.

Behavior and Tactics

Fall Caddis adults don't enjoy sitting on water. They bounce, skitter, and hop. In my experience, they're usually on calm edge waters, up under trees, or they're on fairly brisk water that nudges against the banks. I have seen trout ignore a lot of them, though I don't know why. Wherever you find them, try your imitation on a dead-drift float first. If that fails to prod trout into action, try taking an upstream position, casting downstream, then giving your fly some twitches and even skitters, interspersed with periods of free float.

Known Hatches

See the pupa section. You'll find adult Fall Caddis along the edges of nearly every Western trout creek, stream, and river. You'll find them important on far fewer of them. But the simple dressings are always worth carrying and worth trying when adults are out.

McKenzie Caddis larva

McKenzie Caddis larva

Common names: McKenzie Caddis, Great Gray Spotted Sedge
Latin name: *Arctopsyche grandis*
Size range: #8–12 (17–25 mm, ⅝–1 inch)

Key Features

Case: Net spinner; builds pebble and twig retreat
Anal hooks: Large, on extended process; long tufts of hairs
Body: Large; tan to brown to dark green
Gills: Profuse branched gills
Thorax: Three hardened plates on back

Habitat

This large net-spinning caddis larva lives in heavy flows of freestone riffles and cascades. It builds its retreats in crevices between the largest stones, in the fastest drops, in waterways ranging from headwater streams you can jump across to rivers the size of Montana's Big Hole. It builds nets with meshes of the largest sizes and is most common in small streams and mountain rivers, where debris in the drift is most coarse.

Emergence

Larvae are most important in early to late spring, when they've attained their largest sizes, just before they seal themselves away for pupation. Adults emerge from late May through June and July. Though it's doubtful trout ever feed with true selectivity on these big larvae, they do see a lot of them, and an imitation is rarely refused where the naturals are abundant. The naturals are in the drift often; their habitat lends itself to the Czech nymphing method.

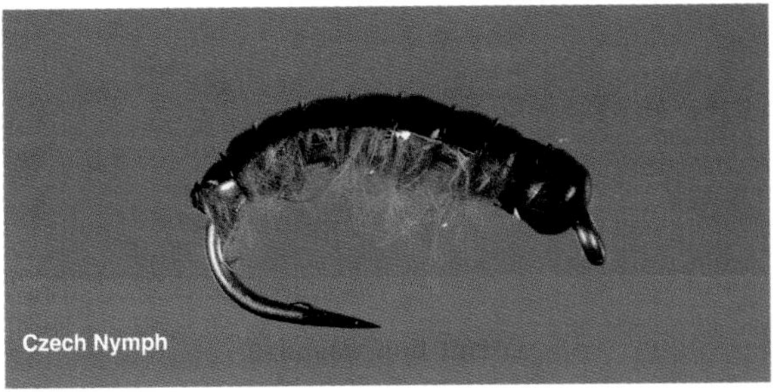
Czech Nymph

Behavior and Tactics

These larvae are tumbled out of their retreats by the currents or voluntarily join the biotic drift to disperse. They are not able to swim and are at the whim of currents until they touch bottom stones. Rig to fish their imitations on the bottom, according to the water depth and current speed. The Czech method calls for a long leader and a three-nymph rig fished with a long rod. Get close to your target and make a short upstream cast, fishing only the long leader that includes a piece of colored monofilament for a sighter. After your flies sink to the bottom, lead them through the drift, maintain a tight line, and watch your sighter for takes.

Known Hatches

McKenzie R., OR; Big Hole R. and both Boulder rivers, MT. Taxonomic references list *A. grandis* as common in AB, BC, CA, CO, ID, MT, OR, UT, WA, and WY. It's listed as present in NM and NV. I collect it most often in bounding headwater streams.

McKenzie Caddis pupa

McKenzie Caddis pupa (Rick Hafele)

Common names: McKenzie Caddis, Great Gray Spotted Sedge pupa
Latin name: *Arctopsyche grandis*
Size range: #6–10 (17–25 mm, 5⁄8–1 inch)

Key Features

Body: Large and portly
Color: Pale to bright green
Wing cases: Gray or brown when mature
Gills: Prominent branched gills on sides of abdomen

Habitat

Pupae are important in the rough waters where the larvae abound. They are found most often in smaller mountain streams, toward the bouldered headwaters, but can also be found in fast riffle and cascade sections of larger rivers, especially where the bottom consists of fairly large rocks. They are most famous on such waters as the Big Hole River in the Rockies and their namesake McKenzie River in Oregon's Cascade Range.

Emergence

These big caddis pupae begin cutting free from their pupal cocoons in late May and early June in the coast, Cascade, and Sierra Mountain ranges and continue through July and even into August or September in the higher parts of the Rocky Mountains. Daily emergence is rumored to be mostly at night, but they've been observed hatching in mid to late afternoon by such careful observers as Arlen Thomason, who writes about the hatch extensively in *BugWater*.

Behavior and Tactics

These large insects are powerful swimmers, but they are still tossed around dramatically on the sorts of brisk currents where they emerge. Your only hint of this happening will usually be the sight of a few adults in the air, though at times you'll also notice the big cast shucks on the water. Always switch to a pupal pattern quickly if a dry fly fails to take trout. Rig it much as you would a dry, but fish it either upstream to rises, sunk, or on a gentle swing, through trout working in riffles and pocketwater.

Known Hatches

Though you might find them important on any Western headwater stream or mountain river, McKenzie Caddis are most famous for their late spring and early summer hatch on Oregon's McKenzie River.

McKenzie Caddis adult

McKenzie Caddis adult

Common names: McKenzie Caddis, Great Gray Spotted Sedge
Latin name: *Arctopsyche grandis*
Size range: #8–12 (17–25 mm, ⅝–1 inch)

Key Features
Body: Large; olive to brownish olive
Wings: Brown, with lighter speckling
Antennae: Approximately body length

Habitat

These big adults hatch in freestone streams, from headwaters downstream to big rivers, always from riffles and even rapids. They are most common in forested mountain areas above 1,500 feet elevation. I've fished them most often on the McKenzie River in Oregon and the Boulder River on the Continental Divide north of Butte, Montana. They're sometimes nocturnal, but they're over streams enough in afternoon that trout are constantly interested in imitations.

Emergence

Hatches are typically in June in the Pacific region, and July in the Rockies. Emergence takes place from midafternoon to after nightfall. Adults are around the stream in afternoon and increasingly at evening. Even if trout fail to feed selectively on the McKenzie Caddis at times, it's such a big, beautiful, and widespread caddis that it's worth knowing what to do about it when you encounter it, which you will.

Behavior and Tactics

This insect will return to the water sporadically throughout its long hatch period, two to three weeks, and trout will see enough during that time to build up a memory of them. The big floating imitation is likely to bring trout up from boisterous water at nearly any time during the day, though they're most useful in evening. It should never be overlooked that such large and heavily-hackled dressings make excellent platforms from which to suspend nymphs, even if they're not imitations of the larva that gives rise to the Great Gray Sedge adult.

Known Hatches

Rather than think in terms of known hatches, you'd be wise to tie a few of the dressings listed for this hatch and carry them with you on your travels to all Western mountain waters. You'll find times to apply them to water.

8 Midges and Crane Flies

Midges and crane flies are at opposite ends of the size spectrum in the insect order Diptera. They have a single pair of wings. The hind pair have evolved into stalked knobs called *halteres*, which are gyroscopes to help stabilize these insects in flight.

Moving-water midges are almost universally small to tiny. A big one is size 16; an average one is closer to size 20; many are size 24 and 26. You find those same sizes in lakes and ponds, where midges are more important, but stillwaters have much larger ones as well (see chapter 15). All Diptera go through complete metamorphosis, with larva, pupa, and adult stages. Midge larvae are eaten constantly by trout in moving water, but they do not meet the criteria for selectivity. Both pupal and adult stages do at times, and you'll need to know when trout are focused on them. Midge pupae are the most important stage of the insect.

Midges have from one to five generations in a year, so they might be important at any time throughout the season. They're about the only thing hatching in winter, so they're often considered the most important insect to trout fishermen at that time of year.

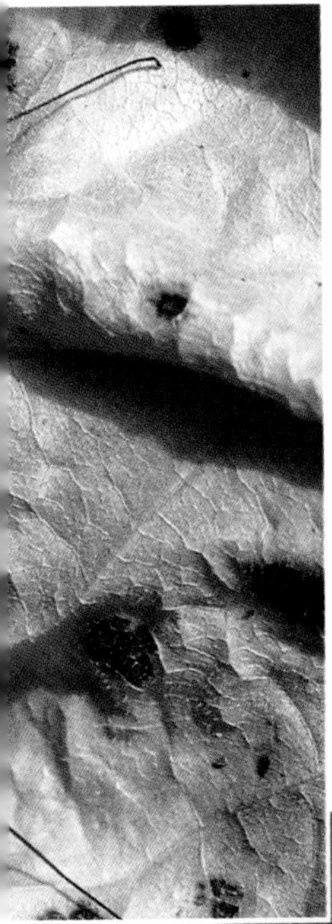

Crane flies are among the largest insects you'll imitate on moving water. The larvae are not only shaped a bit like worms, they also behave a lot like them, burrowing in the silt or gravel of the streambed. Trout see them often enough, and because they're so big, are glad to get them. The adults fly awkwardly just above the surface, with those long legs trailing. Trout sometimes leap to take them in flight.

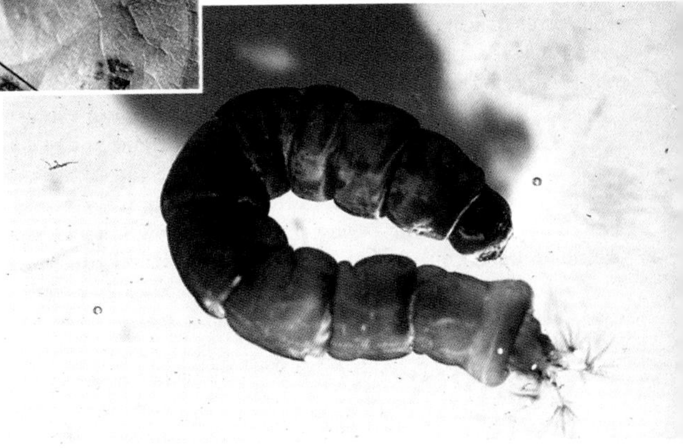

Midge pupa

Common names: Midge, chironomid
Latin name: Chironomidae (more than 50 genera and untold species)
Size range: #16–24 (3–10 mm, ⅛–⅜ inch)

Key Features

Body shape: Slender, tapered, distinctly ribbed
Body color: Dark brown, black, red, green
Wing cases: One pair, short, tucked against abdomen
Thorax: Dark; hunchback-like
Gills: Feathery, at top of thorax and tip of abdomen

Habitat

Midge pupae arise from larvae that live in silt, on vegetation, and on rocks on the stream bottom. They typically build either burrows into the substrate or tubes extending from it. They become more abundant as the current slows and the bottom type becomes more habitable to them. Midge pupae are most important in spring creeks and tailwaters but only important on flats and peaceful pools in freestone streams and rivers.

Emergence

Midges hatch at any time of year, but they're most important in winter, spring, and fall, and are least important in midsummer. Daily hatches are usually from midday into late afternoon. The pupae drift and stage just beneath the surface prior to emergence. Trout hold high in the water and sip the small insects patiently. Takes are often so near the surface that it appears trout are taking adults. But most midges will be taken as pupae, subsurface.

Behavior and Tactics

Midge pupae can swim a bit, but for the most part they rise from bottom to top buoyed by gases trapped between their inner and outer skins. Trout usually feed on them as they drift without much movement, just inches deep, generally on smooth flats, tailouts, or pools. I rig with a pea-size yarn indicator, a small wire nymph for weight on a 20-inch 5X tippet, and then a Thread Midge on another 20-inch tippet, usually 6X. Fish this rig to working trout. Syl's Midge is designed to be fished on a very slow swing to trout feeding visibly.

Known Hatches

Yakima R., WA; Deschutes R. and Fall R., OR; Hat Ck. and Hot Ck., CA; Bow R., AB; Bighorn R. and Missouri R., MT; Silver Ck., ID; Firehole R., WY; Green R., UT; S. Platte R., CO; Colorado R., AZ; San Juan R., NM.

Midge adult

Common names: Midge, chironomid, buzzer
Latin name: Chironomidae (more than 50 genera and untold species)
Size range: #16–24 (3–10 mm, 1/8–3/8 inch)

Key Features

Body shape: Long, slender, tapered
Body color: Black, red, or green
Wings: Single pair, short, held over back
Legs: Long, spindly
Antennae: Males have plumelike tufts; females lack them

Habitat

Though midges emerge in all water types, they're taken selectively in moving water only on smooth flows. You'll fish their imitations most often on spring creeks and tailwaters, and least often on freestone streams. If you find midge patterns useful on freestone waters, it will almost always be on flats, glides, or pools. Streams and rivers with bottoms that are either silted or vegetated produce the heaviest hatches of midges.

Emergence

Midges hatch year-round, but they're most important in late winter through spring and then again in fall and early winter. They often come off in great numbers and form clusters and even rafts on the surface. Trout on calm flows often key on clumps of midges rather than singles. Though you should try a small imitation if you observe trout nipping at individuals, switch to a cluster pattern if the midges are gathered.

Behavior and Tactics

The simple Griffith's Gnat represents a single midge cripple, an adult struggling to get free from the nymphal shuck in the surface film. The Cluster Midge, no more than an Adams with an extra hackle palmered over the body, imitates clusters. Midges emerge on smooth waters and gather in eddies. Trout nose at them patiently. Rig with long, fine tippets, and make delicate presentations without lining the trout. Drag is usually fatal when you're fishing the Griffith's Gnat, but the Cluster Midge will benefit from a bit of movement on the water. Skitter it, and then let it rest.

Known Hatches

I've fished the single Griffith's Gnat on the Paradise Valley spring creeks in Montana and on the Green River below Flaming Gorge Dam in Utah. The Cluster Midge has solved hatches for me on the Cimarron River in New Mexico and on the Madison River below Beartrap Canyon.

Crane fly larva

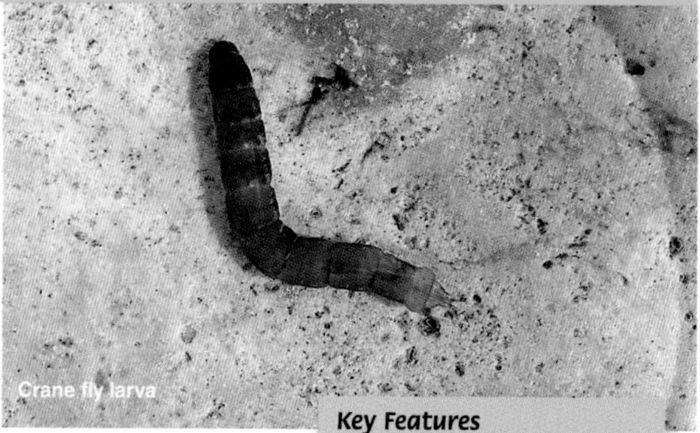

Common name: Crane fly larva
Latin name: Tipulidae (more than 60 genera and 1,400 species in North America)
Size range: #6–10 (12–50 mm, ½–2 inches)

Key Features
Body shape: Cylindrical, wormlike
Gills: None; last segment with two breathing spiracles
Body color: Cream, olive, amber, gray, to dark brown
Head: Dark; usually retracted inside body

Habitat

No attempt is made here to sort crane flies by species or even genera. It's easy to generalize them, and you need only one or two patterns to match them. Crane fly larvae are not all aquatic. Those that are live in all sorts of creeks, streams, and rivers. They burrow beneath the streambed, in gravel or trapped detritus, and are important to imitate only where your collecting reveals large populations.

Emergence

Aquatic crane flies have a one- or two-year life cycle, emerging in spring, summer, or fall. Because of the great number of species, it's likely you'll find larvae in riffle kick net samples at all times of year.

Larvae crawl out of the water; pupation takes place in damp soil along stream margins. The emergence itself is of no importance. Imitation of crane fly larvae should be triggered by collecting and finding them dominant in samples.

Behavior and Tactics

Crane fly larvae cannot swim; when caught on the currents they writhe a bit, but it doesn't result in any significant progress. When trout see them, it will be along the bottom, and they will be either crawling or adrift and protesting. It's likely they look much like an earthworm, and it's possible they're one reason nightcrawlers make such good bait. Rig to fish these big nymph imitations with split shot if necessary to get them to the bottom, and with an indicator. Tumble them dead-drift on or very near the bottom.

Known Hatches

I've collected crane fly larvae from nearly every shallow, gravelly trout stream riffle I've ever kicked around in with a net. This past August I spotted a 3-inch long, nearly black specimen crawling out of the water toward pupation in damp soil alongside the Missouri River tailwater in Montana.

Crane fly adult

Crane fly adult

Common name: Crane fly
Latin name: Tipulidae (more than 60 genera and 1,400 species in North America)
Size range: #12–16 (12–50 mm, ½–2 inches)

Key Features

Body shape: Elongated, clublike
Body color: Tan to dark brown; some with distinct markings
Wings: One pair, about body length
Wing stubs: *Halteres*, knobs on stalks, in place of hindwings
Legs: Very long in relation to body size
Antennae: Short

Habitat

The terrestrial crane fly adults that fly over your lawn and enter your house are the same shape and size as those that trout see over streams and rivers. You'll not often see them in great numbers on or over the water, though it does happen that they get onto the water in sufficient numbers to cause occasional selectivity. It happens more often on tailwaters than freestone or spring streams.

Emergence

Crane flies are most important during the general business of flying around and over trout water. They're awkward flyers. Trout often try for them as they skim the surface. This might happen any time between late spring and early fall, but in my experience it is most common on warm summer days, especially just after light rain. Rather than an exact imitation, it's best to tie flies that represent the adults whirring over the water, touching down to it lightly.

Behavior and Tactics

The spider, and a number of similar dressings listed in tying books as variants, are all designed to sit on the water like thistledown. The color of the pattern is not as important as this lightness. The Hewitt Skater should be fished across and downstream, alternately retrieved like a streamer, but on the surface, and then allowed to sit. It skips and hops and slides. I've had trout jump over it, splash it, bat it out of the way, and then finally engulf it. It's fun to fish. It behaves a lot like a crane fly adult hovering over the water.

Known Hatches

I've had the most fun fishing spiders and skaters in remote and less than heavily fished waters. I've used them most often to excite trout into striking in bright sunshine on days when nothing else would move them.

9 Terrestrials

Terrestrials arrive on water from the opposite direction as aquatics: They migrate by accident from shore or get wafted onto the water by gusts of wind. Some, such as grasshoppers, land on water through miscalculation of their own ability to maintain controlled flight: Their legs propel them into the air over water, but their wings are not strong enough to keep them airborne.

Stream banks are a transition line between aquatic and terrestrial environments. Aquatic insects migrate across the streambed toward shore. Terrestrial insects fall to the water next to shore from grasses and bushes. Trout line up in good bank water and are fed doubly, from both directions. If any single terrestrial insect becomes most abundant, those trout become selective to it.

Beetles, ants, and grasshoppers are the most important terrestrial insects, because trout are most likely to feed selectively on them. Other terrestrials reach occasional, but not common, significance. These include leafhoppers, crickets, inchworms, and even stinkbugs. Given a chance, a trout will consume any of these. But they'll rarely see enough of them at one time to become selective. If trout do focus on a peripheral terrestrial insect in your home waters, however, you need to collect it and track down imitations for it.

It's said that trout have a preference for the taste of ants. I have no reason to contest this. It's true that a trout will often turn aside for an ant imitation when it seems to be feeding exclusively on BWO or PMD duns or anything else and there is not an ant in sight. The same can be said of beetle imitations: Trout take them even in the total absence of naturals. Perhaps it's because trout see so many of these terrestrials, so constantly. For whatever reason, ant and beetle dressings are among your best choices for mismatching a hatch or for fishing over selective rising trout at any time, even if it seems that neither is on the trout menu at the moment.

Inchworms, stinkbugs, and crickets are among the terrestrial insects that trout take as targets of opportunity, but they rarely get a chance to feed on them selectively. Though imitations for them are not listed in this book, it's not difficult to track them down if you find one of these insects the focus of trout on one of your own home waters.

Terrestrial beetle

Terrestrial beetle

Common name: Beetle
Latin name: Coleoptera
Size range: #6–22
(3–20 mm, 1/8–3/4 inch)

Key Features

Tails: None
Wings: Forewings hardened, folded over back
Body shape: Long and slender to round and portly
Body color: Bright red to black
Antennae: About body length

Habitat

Terrestrial beetles fall to the water on brisk freestone streams as often as they do on peaceful spring creeks, but they're most important on waters where the currents are calm. If the stream is small, and the trees tall, they might be fed on selectively by trout all across the currents. Usually they're taken selectively along the edges. I've also fished them around the shores of lakes and ponds.

Emergence

Beetles are most important in the warmth of late spring, summer, and early fall. They're most active midday, when the sun is warmest. Whenever you see trout sipping along edge waters, suspect beetles. Even if that's not what they're taking, they'll accept a beetle imitation most of the time. Beetles vary in size from too tiny to imitate to too large to be convenient to cast. The most useful imitations run from size 14 through 20.

Behavior and Tactics

Beetles on water often struggle with their legs and wings and give out a sequence of tiny concentric waves that probably trigger many takes by trout. But I've never figured out how to imitate this, so I fish beetle patterns dead-drift. They're at their best when presented delicately, on fine tippets, to picky trout working along grassy edges. They're often the key to fooling trout that everybody else is trying with mayfly, caddis, or other imitations. Though our province in this chapter is streams, a Black Foam Beetle often works wonders on lakes and ponds.

Known Hatches

Beetles should always be in your fly boxes and should always come out when you get into trout that are rising, and selective to something, but you're unable to solve that something with any other imitations. Fall back on a beetle dressing.

Terrestrial ant

Ant

Common names: Ant and winged ant
Latin name: Formicidae
Size range: #12–22 (3–12 mm, ⅛–⅞ inch)

Key Features

Body shape: Hourglass; large abdomen, narrow thorax, large head
Body color: Brown to black
Winged ants: Wings held flat over back; extend beyond body
Antennae: Shorter than body

Habitat

Ants leave their nests and explore their territories for food. Their foraging often takes them to the edges of water, where they fall in or get blown in by gusting winds. The non-winged variety are only important along stream edges, and usually on smooth water. Bank-feeding trout are suckers for small ant patterns fished tight to grasses and shrubs. Winged ants are often delivered out away from banks, on both streams and stillwaters, where trout appreciate them highly.

Emergence

Most ants lack wings and are important all through the warmth of late spring and summer. Dispersal flights of winged ants take to the air in search of new territories, in my experience most often in May and June. Their flights commonly end on water, whether in streams and rivers or in lakes and ponds. Trout feed on them on the surface and submerged. Both winged and wingless ants are most important in the warmest parts of the day.

Behavior and Tactics

Ants have waxy bodies that repel water. Floating patterns should ride low in the surface film. It's no secret that many ants are taken by trout sunk. A fur ant, winged or wingless, is excellent when fished as a wet fly. Fish it along the banks on an upstream cast and dead-drift presentation. If lots of winged ants are in the air over a stream, fish a sunk imitation on a slow swing. If you notice even a few winged ants over a lake or pond, try a winged wet imitation fished on a very slow retrieve.

Known Hatches

Ant patterns are famous for working on such smooth tailwaters and spring creeks as the Henrys Fork of the Snake in Idaho, the Bow River in Alberta, and the Bighorn River in Montana. Try them whenever you can't solve rising trout with anything else.

Grasshopper

Common names: Grasshopper, hopper
Latin name: Orthoptera
Size range: #6–14 (10–40 mm, ½–1½ inches)

Key Features

Body shape: Cylindrical and blocky
Body color: Tan, olive, yellow, brown, or gray
Legs: Hind legs thick and strong, for jumping
Wings: Short and feeble to long and powerful
Head: Blocky, blunt

Habitat

Grasshoppers are primarily insects of grasslands, but they're found, and become important to trout, wherever grasses approach near the edges of streams. I've found them just as critical to my fishing on streams and rivers that flow through open forest, with grass growing beneath the trees, as I have on pastorals. Modern spraying of insecticides has reduced their importance on some waters where they were once the dominant summer fare for trout.

Emergence

Hoppers leave the egg in spring, grow through summer, and reach maturity in late summer or early fall. They're most important when they're most abundant and most active. That coincides with the heat of summer and the browning of grasses alongside streams. It's wise to start with a small size 12 or 14 hopper in early summer, progressing to larger patterns as the naturals increase in size. Observe hopper colors carefully. Some are bright yellow; most are much more drab.

Behavior and Tactics

Hoppers are awkward flyers; they're as likely to land on water as on land. When they do, it's often with a smack. Their flights are not always short. Though more of them are taken along the banks than farther out, it's not always wise to restrict fishing hopper imitations to the edges. Trout twenty and thirty feet out from the banks see enough hoppers to know what to do about the next one that lands near them. Hoppers protest their presence on water; if a dead-drift float doesn't bring trout up for you, try a bit of skate.

Known Hatches

Listing rivers famous for grasshopper fishing might cause you to restrict your fishing unnecessarily. I use them on small and medium size streams more often than I do on big, famous rivers. They should have a permanent place in your fly boxes.

10 Crustaceans

Three types of crustaceans are fed on selectively, at times, by trout in moving water: scuds, aquatic sow bugs, and crayfish. None of these are *hatches* as such, but all attract the focus of trout to such an extent that you should have imitations of each in your fly boxes. Crustaceans have no aerial stage. They're present in water at all times, available to trout, and are often considered most important when aquatic and terrestrial insects, with their cyclic availability, are not clamoring for the selective attentions of trout. Crustaceans in streams are usually most important in late fall, winter, and early spring.

Scuds feed on vegetation or decaying detritus. They're prime candidates for imitation wherever plants take root in moving water, usually in spring creeks and tamed tailwaters. They're least important in freestone streams, though you'll find them in marginal edge waters, just inches deep and with little flow, where trout rarely feed. They're very important in lakes and ponds (see chapter 19).

Aquatic sow bugs are only important in tailwaters and a few spring creeks where flows are so stable and gentle that vegetation grows in thick carpets right on bottom rocks. This is often mistakenly called *moss*. It can be loaded with sow bugs on such waters as the Bighorn River in Montana, downstream from Yellowtail Dam. I've never seen sow bugs in more than scattered numbers in freestone streams.

Crayfish are omnivores, feeding mostly on trapped detrital vegetation, but also on whatever animal matter they're able to find already dead and decaying, or even alive but too small or too slow to escape. Crayfish live in all water types, moving and still, but are most abundant, and most important, in rocky freestone streams where flows are not fast. They're most often fed on by trout along stream edges, on pool tailouts, or down the length of fairly slow runs.

Scuds

Aquatic sow bugs

Crayfish

Scuds, aquatic sow bugs, and crayfish are all crustaceans, and are all fed on selectively at certain times, and in specific water types, by trout. If you fish waters where they're prevalent, you should carry imitations, and know when to fish them.

Scud

Scuds

Common names: Scud, sideswimmer
Latin name: Amphipoda
Size range: #10–16 (5–20 mm, ⅜–¾ inch)

Key Features

Body shape: Flattened side to side; hardened back
Body color: Light gray to olive or brown
Abdomen: Six segments, each with a pair of swimmer paddles
Thorax: Seven segments, each with a pair of legs
Antennae: Two pairs, about equal in length

Habitat

Scuds are most important in tailwaters and spring creeks stable enough to allow vegetation to take root. They also scuttle over and in silted streambeds, where trout feed on them heavily. I've had my best fishing over scuds in tailwaters used for irrigation during periods when flows are reduced in late fall, winter, and early spring. Trout become selective to them when other foods are not easily available.

Emergence

There is no emergence of scuds. They never leave the water and are available to trout at all seasons of the year. Trout might feed on them selectively during any month, at any time of day. If you're on the type of water that has attached plants, scoop a handful of vegetation from the water, lay it out in the sun, and watch what materializes out of it. Most of the time it will be scuds about the color of the vegetation.

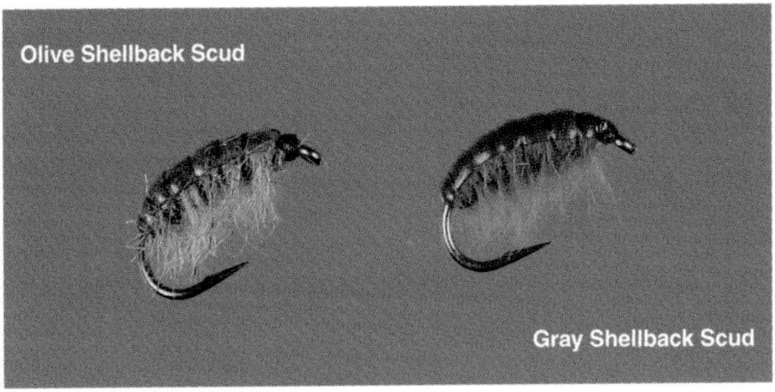

Behavior and Tactics

Scuds spend all their lives in and around vegetation or over and in silt bottoms. When at rest in the water, on vegetation, or in the palm of your hand, scuds will be curved. When they swim briskly, which we must assume they do when a trout is chasing them, they straighten out and look much like little animated sticks. You can tie your imitations on curved or straight hooks. Either way, rig to fish them at the depths of the vegetation or bottom on which they live. Present them dead-drift or on a slow swing.

Known Hatches

More lakes than streams are famous for scuds. But you'll find them in most Western tailwaters and spring creeks, the requirement for selective feeding being gentle and stable flows. Many little-known and small tailwaters should be famous for them.

Aquatic sow bug

Aquatic sow bug

Common names: Sow bug, cress bug
Latin name: Isopoda
Size range: #14–20 (5–20 mm, ⅜–¾ inch)

Key Features

Body shape: Flattened top to bottom; wider at back than head
Body color: Gray to brown or black
Abdomen: Fused into one segment; forked tail-like appendages
Thorax: Seven segments, each with a pair of legs
Antennae: Two pairs; one pair much longer than other

Habitat

Aquatic sow bugs are cryptic bottom dwellers. Though adapted most commonly to very shallow ponds and seeps and backwaters—non-trout habitats—they live in moving waters where bottom rocks are covered with the attached vegetation that we usually call moss. They're important in a few spring creeks but more often in tailwaters that are not flushed so heavily that aquatic vegetation is wiped out.

Emergence

Aquatic sow bugs have no emergence period. They're in the water in all months of the year, at all times of day. They're most important when no hatches draw trouts' attention. Trout hanging over close crops of vegetation on bottom stones likely see more aquatic sowbugs than any other food form. I've often caught trout during hatches, taken throat samples, and noticed signs of earlier selective feeding on sow bugs. A small imitation is almost always a good choice on a tailwater.

Behavior and Tactics

Sow bugs are very poor swimmers. When caught in the currents, they drift helplessly. You'll almost always fish their imitations in slow to moderate currents with even depths and constant velocities. It's the ideal situation to rig with a hinged leader and a substantial yarn indicator, with putty weight or split shot added as needed to get the nymph to the bottom. Most often, sow bug imitations are used as small trailing patterns, ten to twelve inches behind a San Juan Worm or larger scud dressing. Always fish them dead-drift.

Known Hatches

Bow R., AB; Bighorn R., MT; San Juan R., NM. This minimal list gives you an idea of the type of water where sow bugs are important. The small imitations tied for them are effective everywhere, whether sow bugs are dominant in the system or not.

Crayfish

Common names: Crayfish, crawdad
Latin name: Decapoda
Size range: #4–12 (10–150 mm, ½–6 inches)

Key Features

Body shape: Lobster-like; front half round, back half flattened
Body color: Olive-brown to bright red
Legs: Four pairs of walking legs
Claws: Front pair of legs enlarged into claws

Habitat

Crayfish are most abundant in Pacific coastal states and provinces, and rare to absent in many Rocky Mountain waters. They're found in all types of water, both moving and still. They spend most of their time hiding under bottom rocks or logs or in decaying debris such as leaf packs. They're most important in freestone streams and tailwaters, where they prowl stream edges and tailouts of pools.

Emergence

Crayfish do not emerge; they're present in streams and rivers at all times of year. They're nocturnal, crawling along the bottom to scavenge whatever plant and animal matter they encounter. Their tendency to forage at night predicts daily periods of importance at first and last light. Though I've seen only occasional evidence that trout feed selectively on them, I've found so many in trout stomach samples that it's clear trout rarely pass up a chance at one.

Behavior and Tactics

The simple Girdle Bug is impressionistic; Bob Clouser's wonderful crayfish is more imitative. The colors of either can be varied to match crayfish in your own waters. I recently collected dozens of half- to one-inch crayfish from the Missouri River near Craig, Montana, that were pale, almost ghostlike. Pay attention to these differences. When startled, crayfish flip their paddles to swim backward, claws trailing. They can move swiftly. Fish imitations as streamers if you're after big trout on the hunt in the shallows. In deeper water, try dead-drifting them near the bottom.

Known Hatches

Strangely, biologists report crayfish are common everywhere, except that they're not found in most of the western Great Plains and Rocky Mountains. A quick computer search of my own collection records reveals only one noted instance of crayfish in the Rockies, on the Missouri River in Montana.

11 Aquatic Worms

Aquatic Worm

Common names:
Aquatic earthworm, wriggler
Latin name: Annelida
Size range: #10–18
(10–50 mm, ½–2 inches)

Key Features
Body shape: Slender, elongate, cylindrical
Body color: Tan to flesh-colored to red
Tails/head/legs: All absent

Habitat

Aquatic worms are most common in the silt and sand of spring creek and tailwater substrates. They also burrow into sand and gravel trapped in freestone riffles and can be found on rocks in stable currents, where stone faces are carpeted by beds of close-cropped plants. They are common in mature rivers, and less common in headwater areas. They're also found in lakes and ponds but are not often dislodged and exposed to trout.

Emergence

Aquatic worms have no hatch cycle and are never absent from streams and rivers. Because they live in the top few inches of most bottom *soils*, they could be said to emerge just after a spate has stirred that stew. But they're fed on selectively only where bottom conditions for them are perfect and populations are dense, mostly in silt-bottomed tailwaters. Some aquatic worms have hemoglobin for oxygen absorption; these are red, and many imitations are based on them.

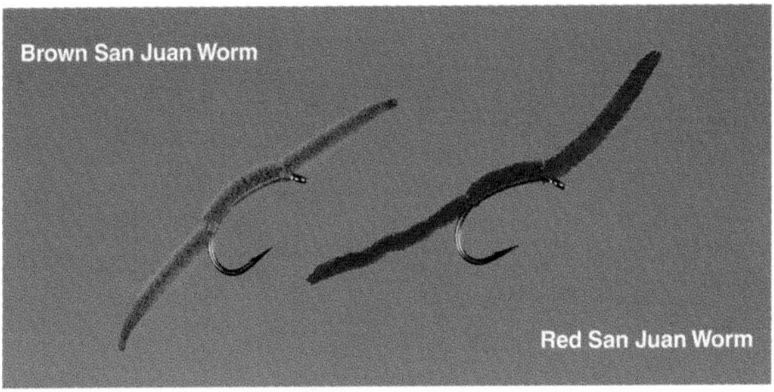

Behavior and Tactics

Aquatic worms do not swim. They're always taken on or near the bottom. Rig to fish your imitations in that zone, using an indicator to tell you about takes, and sufficient weight, depending on water depth and current speed, to get them there. On heavily-fished tailwaters such as the San Juan River in New Mexico, trout will accept them gently. Use the most delicate rig you can, with little weight and a very buoyant indicator. Set the hook at the least quiver. You'll rarely get the kind of strike that yanks your indicator under.

Known Hatches

Elk R., BC; Yakima R., WA; Malhuer R., OR; Fall R., CA; Bow R., AB; Bighorn R., MT; Wind R., WY; Strawberry R., UT; Colorado R., CO; San Juan R., NM; Truckee R., NV; Black R., AZ.

12 Sculpins

Sculpin

Common name: Sculpin
Latin name: Cottidae
Size range: #2–12
(25–150 mm, 1–6 inches)

Key Features

Body shape: Broad head, tapering to narrow at tail
Body color: Drab olive to brown; often mottled
Fins: Large, fanlike pectorals; large dorsal and anal fins

Habitat

Sculpins are most important in stream and river flows over beds of clean gravel and cobble. In my early days of enjoying trout for streamside dinners, I found sculpins in trout stomachs from brisk headwater streams to mature freestone rivers. They hide along the bottom, hugging stones in riffles, at stream and river edges, and on tailouts of pools, darting from place to place when disturbed.

Emergence

The sculpin life cycle lasts from one to several years; they're always present in rivers and streams. If they have any moment of most importance, it's when brown trout get restless in fall, making spawning runs out of reservoirs or just becoming more active as their urges move them. Daily importance is at dawn and dusk, but only because big trout tend to go on the prowl for big bites, in shallow water, during those hours of low light.

Behavior and Tactics

In my experience, sculpin imitations on the small side, size 6 to 10 rather than 2 and 4, are easier to cast and catch just as many trout and sufficient large ones. Sculpins dart in swift bursts when disturbed. Most of the time imitations should be fished as the streamers that they are, either with a swimming motion animated by a downstream swing or a stripping retrieve that scoots them along in darts. In some situations, usually just downstream from dam releases, trout take crippled sculpins, and you should tumble your imitation along the bottom, dead-drift.

Known Hatches

Sculpins are simply everywhere in the West. You should always be armed with a few imitations. I use them most often when floating big rivers, fishing them between places to anchor and look for rising trout.

PART THREE

Western Stillwater Hatches

13 Mayflies

Speckle-Wing nymph

Speckle-Wing nymph

Common names: Speckle-Wing nymph, Speckle-Wing Quill nymph, *Callibaetis*

Latin names: *Callibaetis ferrugineus* and *C. pictus* (7 related species)

Size range: #12–18 (6–12 mm, ¼–½ inch)

Key Features

Tails: Three, equal length, fringed with hairs

Gills: Large, on abdominal segments

Body color: Olive to olive-brown, tan, or gray

Antennae: Long; half body length or longer

Habitat

Speckle-Wings are primarily stillwater mayflies, though populations can be found in vegetated spring creeks, such as Silver Creek in Idaho. They're found in nearly every Western lake, pond, and reservoir and are the most important stillwater mayfly. Nymphs thrive in rooted vegetation and can also be found foraging on photosynthetic bottom growth and decaying matter. They're abundant in shallows, on shoals, and in plant beds at any depth.

Emergence

Callibaetis have three generations each year. The first is in spring; the second, hatching from eggs laid by the first, in mid-summer; and the third in autumn. The nymphs of each generation are a size smaller than those of the one before it, usually size 12 in spring, 14 in summer, and 16 in fall. Nymph imitations are important in the weeks before hatches, as searching patterns, and during a hatch, when trout feed heavily on them as they swim up for emergence.

Behavior and Tactics

These swimmer mayfly nymphs flit from place to place in plants or along the bottom. Fish their imitations along shorelines, in weedy coves or shallows, over shoals or plant beds close to shore or far from it, and over the bottom wherever sunlight reaches it and promotes photosynthetic growth. Use a line that reaches the depth you need, and then fish these nymphs on a hand-twist retrieve, alternating with a few short, sharp strips. Fish them shallow during a hatch, either on a stripping retrieve or suspended beneath an indicator or dry fly.

Known Hatches

Kamloops-area lakes, BC; Chopaka Lk., WA; Hosmer Lk., OR; Manzanita Lk. and Martis Ck. Res., CA; Georgetown and Hebgen Lks., MT; Yellowstone Lk., WY; Henrys Lk., ID; Strawberry Res., UT; Delaney Butte Lks., CO; Ruby Lks., NV; Eagle Nest Lk., NM; Sunrise Lk., AZ.

Speckle-Wing dun

Speckle-Wing dun

Common names: Speckle-Wing dun, *Callibaetis* dun
Latin names: *Callibaetis ferrugineus* and *C. pictus* (7 related species)
Size range: #12–18 (6–12 mm, ¼–½ inch)

Key Features

Tails: Two
Body: Olive-brown to gray on back; light olive-tan to olive-gray on belly
Wings: Mottled
Hindwings: Very small and elliptical
Eyes: Male eyes large, divided

Habitat

Speckle-Wing dun hatches are generally associated with shallow, weed-filled waters. They'll always hatch there, and it's the first place to look for them on any lake or pond. But their nymphs also live on shoals and plant beds, sometimes far from shore, or on any bottom that is not too deep to have plant growth. You'll find Speckle-Wing duns hatching above such habitats, often far from shore.

Emergence

Spring, summer, and fall hatches of *Callibaetis* duns are roughly in April and May, June and July, and September and October. On each body of water, each hatch will last two to four weeks, with a two-week peak, and then a lull before the next generation emerges. Daily emergence is in the warmest part of the day, early to late afternoon, in spring and fall. The summer hatch might be pushed toward morning or evening. Emergence takes place in the surface film.

Behavior and Tactics

Speckle-Wings usually have enough mass to break through the surface film in a hurry, but the dun takes from a few seconds to almost a minute to escape the nymphal shuck, making an emerger dressing valuable. Duns sit on the water for a short time in warm weather; longer in rain or cool weather. Trout feed on them heavily, sometimes focusing on emergers, other times on perfect duns. It's wise to remember that trout take nymphs at a ratio of about ten to one during a *Callibaetis* emergence. It's a reason to suspend a nymph if trout refuse dries.

Known Hatches

Many famous hatches are listed in the nymph section, but you would be foolish not to be prepared for this mayfly if you fish lakes, ponds, or weedy spring creeks anywhere in the West. Speckle-Wings hatch everywhere and are the most important insect to trout whenever they do.

Speckle-Wing spinner

Common names: Speckle-Wing spinner, Speckle-Wing Quill, *Callibaetis* spinner
Latin names: *Callibaetis ferrugineus* and *C. pictus* (7 related species)
Size range: #12–18 (6–12 mm, ¼–½ inch)

Key Features

Tails: Two, white or light gray
Body color: Back, gray or brown; underside, pale tan or gray
Wings: Male, clear; female, mottled with black or brown
Hindwings: Small, elliptical
Eyes: Male eyes large, split

Habitat

Male *Callibaetis* form swarms in afternoon over lakes and ponds, but it's females that land on water, lay their eggs, and get eaten by trout. Spinnerfalls happen in association with the same habitats listed for the nymphs and duns: along the shoreline, above shallows, and over shoals and plant beds farther from shore. Watch for feeding trout during a *Callibaetis* spinnerfall and fish for them wherever you find them.

Emergence

Spinnerfalls usually happen in late afternoon and early evening, following the hatch of duns. At times the flight of males will form while duns still emerge. It's common for them to attempt to mate an immature female dun. It's not always easy to notice female spinners on the water. Trout don't feed during every spinnerfall, even if it's heavy. Perhaps they're sated by nymphs and duns. Some days, though, they'll focus on spinners and take them eagerly and selectively.

Behavior and Tactics

Female *Callibaetis* spinners fall to the water semi-spent but soon expend all of their energy and lie spent, with their wings flattened in the surface. Trout take them in both postures. The Gulper Special is designed to fish when trout travel high in the water, feeding heavily on Speckle-Wing spinners, or duns as well, gulping down insect after insect. If you can predict the place for the next rise, and set your imitation in the right spot, a trout is likely to take it, unless another natural is so near that the trout fails to notice your fly.

Known Hatches

Important spinnerfalls take place wherever Speckle-Wing dun hatches are moderate to heavy. After you fish through any emergence, stick around and wait for the spinnerfall to see if it gets trout working. Some will, and some won't. You can't predict it.

Hex nymph

Common names: Hex, Big Yellow May, Michigan Caddis
Latin name: *Hexagenia limbata*
Size range: #6–12 (12–37 mm, ½–1½ inches)

Key Features

Tails: Three, shorter than body, fringed with hairs
Body: Yellowish brown, with dark markings on back
Gills: Feathery rows, on abdomen, held above back
Wing cases: Present, prominent
Head: Visible pair of tusks

Habitat

These big nymphs live two years, most of it spent in U-shaped burrows dug into clay or firm mud bottoms. Though they live mostly in lakes and ponds, they're also found in streams and rivers that have appropriate bottoms for tunneling, almost always spring creeks or meadow reaches of freestone streams. Their distribution in the West is patchy, and they are important only in a few scattered locations.

Emergence

Hex nymphs leave their burrows to forage across the bottom only after dark. They're important only during an emergence; though trout in waters with heavy populations might take an imitation at any time of day or season, it's not certain they'd be taking it for a Hex nymph. Emergences in the varied West take place from May through October. Nymph patterns are important in the early period of a hatch, almost always in the last hour before dark.

Behavior and Tactics

Hex nymphs are strong and swift swimmers. At emergence they make bold dashes for the top, from a foot to ten feet or more deep. You can fish their imitations on sinking-tip or clear intermediate lines, but the nymphs are not as important as duns, and you don't want to be caught restringing with a floating line when duns begin to pop. If you can carry two rods, rig one for the nymph and one for the dry. Otherwise, fish the nymph on your floating line, with a stripping retrieve.

Known Hatches

Spokane R. and Merrill Lk., WA; Williamson R., OR; Fall R., CA. Western hatches of this big mayfly have been very poorly cataloged, possibly because they happen at night, but probably because they're worth keeping secret.

Hex dun

Common names: Hex, Big Yellow May, Michigan Caddis
Latin name: *Hexagenia limbata*
Size range: #6–8 (16–37 mm, ¾–1½ inches)

Key Features

Tails: Two, about body length, dark
Body color: Tan to yellow, with dark markings
Wings: Large, pale tan to yellow
Hindwings: Large, similar in shape to forewings

Habitat

Hex duns hatch only over the bottom types demanded by the nymphs from which they arise. On large lakes, they'll be found in shoreline and shoal areas, not at depths more than twenty-five feet or so, where oxygen levels taper away at certain times of year, and the nymphs cannot survive. On streams and rivers they'll hatch all across the currents, usually on placid meadow-stream flows, but never over rocky bottoms.

Emergence

Hex hatches begin in May in California, progress through June and July in most areas, and end in August, September, and even early October at the most northerly latitudes. Daily emergence begins at dusk or just after dark. Under a dense cloud cover, it might begin a bit earlier. In my own experience over the hatch, a few duns begin to emerge, and a few trout begin to feed on them, while you can still see it happening. Then the light is gone, and you fish by the sound of rises rather than sight of them. It's exciting!

Yellow Paradrake

Behavior and Tactics

Hex duns simply sit on the water, once in a while struggling to lift off. You can see them looming in the blackness, like big yellow sailboats, usually becalmed on the water. Trout take them with splashes; if you can't see where to cast, calculate the correct direction by sound. It's better to let your big dry sit than to paste it into every rise ring. Trout become frantic during a good hatch; avoid the same mistake. If trout take naturals near your imitation, give it a bit of a scoot to get their attention.

Known Hatches

See nymph section. I suspect there are more unknown than known Western hatches of this big insect. Most of us leave the water before a hatch would manifest itself. I advise spending some late evenings on your favorite stillwaters, seeing what might develop.

Hex spinner

Common names: Hex, Big Yellow May Spinners, Michigan Caddis
Latin name: *Hexagenia limbata*
Size range: #6–8 (16–37 mm, ¾–1½ inches)

Key Features

Tails: Two, body length or longer, dark
Body color: Tan to yellow-brown, with dark markings
Wings: Large, clear, with dark veins
Hindwings: Large, similar in shape to forewings

Habitat

Hex spinners are important only where hatches of duns are heavy. The spinnerfall is only fishable on waters where it's legal to fish after dark. Most Western states allow it, but my home state, Oregon, is one that does not. The spinner opportunity comes in relation to the shoreline, and its attendant shallows, on most lakes. On streams, spinners will fall to the water on broad flats and pools.

Emergence

Spinners begin to fall as the duns taper off. This will usually be from total darkness to an hour or more after dark, though on occasion they begin a bit earlier. There might be days when the dun hatch fails to materialize, or is slight, but spinners of previous days return to the water to lay their eggs. It's possible to fish the Hex spinnerfall with the same dressing used for the dun.

Big Yellow May Spinner

Behavior and Tactics

Polly Rosborough, the late originator of this spinner dressing, fished the hatch often on his home Williamson River. His prescription was to keep nymph, dun, and spinner dressings on pre-tied, looped tippets. He would start with the nymph, switch quickly to a dun when they appeared, and then make the final switch to the spinner when trout made the same transition. It's not bad advice. When you fish the spinner, try it on a dead float. But it will be night; try scooting it a bit to attract trout and to keep a tight line so you can feel takes.

Known Hatches

Same as those listed for nymphs. I have collected these from the estuary of the Columbia River, where sea-run cutts feed on them. Be on the watch for them, and it's likely you'll extend the known hatches into some areas that nobody else knows about.

14 Caddisflies

Cinnamon Sedge larva

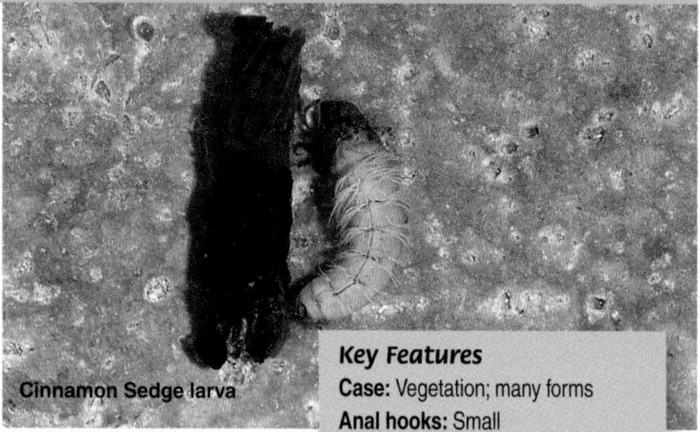

Common names: Cinnamon Sedge, Cinnamon Autumn Sedge, Summer Flier Sedge
Latin name: *Limnephilus* (about 80 species in the West)
Size range: #10–14 (12–25 mm, ½–1 inch)

Key Features
Case: Vegetation; many forms
Anal hooks: Small
Gills: Profuse, branched

Note: The family Limnephilidae has more than 30 Western genera; the genus *Limnephilus*, about 80 Western species. It's an unruly group. Just match them as vegetation-cased caddis.

Habitat

Though they're sometimes found in the marginal areas of streams, Cinnamon Sedges are most important to anglers in lakes and ponds. The larvae clamber about in vegetation or along the bottom. With such a great number of species, they're found in all stillwater habitats, but you'll find the larvae important only along vegetated edges and over plant beds. They're present at all elevations and latitudes, wherever you find weedy shallows.

Emergence

In the larval stage there is no emergence as such. In my experience the larvae are fed on with mild selectivity and become worth imitating only when large numbers of them lose their grip on vegetation and slowly float to the surface. Trout cruise and pluck them like fat, ripe fruits hanging from branches. The swirls are large and look like surface takes, but they're not. It can happen in spring or summer, at any time of day.

Behavior and Tactics

Vegetation-cased caddis in lakes and ponds sometimes miscalculate their specific densities and float to the surface rather than sink to the bottom when they lose their grip. When at the surface they're helpless and try to crawl along it, legs flailing. When more than a few do this, trout become aware of it. Your imitation should reflect the insect, case and all, and should be designed to float in or just under the surface. Cast to cover rising trout or give it the slowest retrieve you can achieve.

Known Hatches

I've fished these imitations on small, heavily-vegetated ponds all over the West. If you adventure into those kinds of waters, the listed dressings will come in handy at times. If you fish them on sinking lines, they make fine dragonfly nymph imitations as well.

Cinnamon Sedge pupa

Cinnamon Sedge pupa

Common names: Cinnamon Sedge, Cinnamon Autumn Sedge, Summer Flier Sedge
Latin name: *Limnephilus* (about 80 species in the West)
Size range: #8–12 (12–25 mm, ½–1 inch)

Key Features

Body: Ginger to brown; dark fringe on abdomen
Gills: Profuse, branched
Wing cases: Brown; darker than body

Note: With such a large group, it's acceptable to just note the size and color, select an imitation, and get on with your fishing without any attempt at recognition or identification.

Habitat

Limnephilus pupae are widespread, but most common, and most important to anglers, over lake and pond waters that are fairly shallow and well-vegetated. Though you'll usually observe these pupae emerging in relation to the shoreline, I've seen them swimming near the surface and far from shore in large British Columbia lakes. It doesn't take many insects of such large size to arouse the interest of trout.

Emergence

Hatches in a group with eighty species can happen in any month, May through October. No general hatch chart will help you; it's necessary to watch for them on your own waters. Daily emergence will be in the midday hours early and late in the season, but will be pushed toward morning and evening in midsummer. Emergence is usually spread out over a two- to three-week period on any given water.

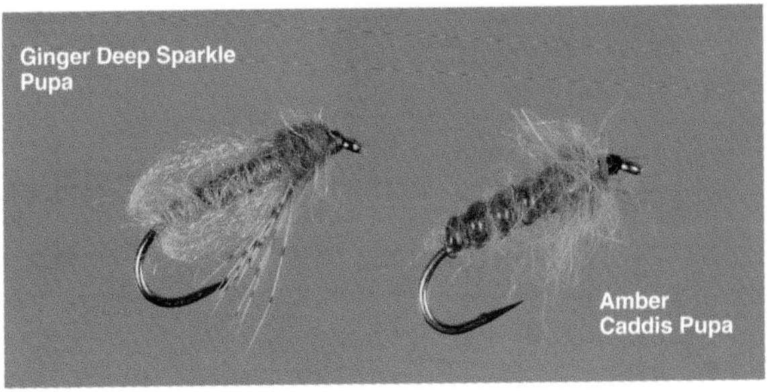

Behavior and Tactics

Some mature Cinnamon Sedge pupae swim to the surface and emerge at once. Many others stroke all the way to shore, sometimes just inches beneath the surface. On the way toward the top they swim briskly. For the first kind, rig with a floating line and long leader or a sink-tip line and shorter leader. Fish your imitation on the rise, without any hesitation. Those that make the longer swim to shore get tuckered out, swimming patiently but feebly. Rig with a clear intermediate line, and use a slow but steady retrieve.

Known Hatches

This large group hatches on all stillwaters. They're most important on weedy ponds but also emerge from large but fairly shallow lakes, wherever sunlight strikes the bottom and promotes the growth of rooted vegetation.

Cinnamon Sedge adult

Cinnamon Sedge adult

Common names: Cinnamon Sedge, Cinnamon Autumn Sedge, Summer Flier Sedge
Latin name: *Limnephilus* (about 80 species in the West)
Size range: #8–12 (12–25 mm, ½–1 inch)

Key Features

Body color: Ginger to amber or brown
Wings: Tan to brown; sometimes mottled
Antennae: About body length

Note: Unless you're a taxonomist, there is little to separate the genera of Limnephilidae. If you see large, ginger to brown caddisflies over any stillwater, match them by size and color.

Habitat

Limnepilus adults are found on all lakes and ponds, usually in association with the vegetated shallows preferred by their larvae. They'll be along the shorelines, rarely in any great abundance, but often in sufficient numbers to get trout interested in an imitation. When trout cruise along reed edges, in coves, or over bottoms with tangled fallen logs, they're susceptible to a floating imitation of a Cinnamon Sedge adult.

Emergence

Hatches are spread out over the entire trout fishing season. Cinnamon Sedge numbers are rarely great, but they're so large that it doesn't take many to make trout notice. Daily emergence is often during mid to late afternoon or evening. Pupal patterns are more important during the emergence itself. Adults are most important when they return to the water to lay their eggs, which can occur at any time of day and might happen most often at night.

Behavior and Tactics

Adult Cinnamon Sedges leave the water quickly at emergence. When they return to the water to lay their eggs, they are restless, batting around above the water, smacking into it, trying to shake off their eggs. Always try your imitations first with a presentation on the sit, casting either to rises or to the plotted place you expect the next rise from a cruising trout. If a float without movement fails, try skating the fly for a few inches and then letting it sit again. You might incite a detonation.

Known Hatches

I know of no famous hatches of the Cinnamon Sedge, but I have encountered it in fairly scattered numbers wherever I've fished stillwaters in the West. It's one that I don't usually carry imitations to match specifically unless I find it important.

Traveling Sedge pupa

Traveling Sedge pupa (Jim Schollmeyer)

Common names: Traveler Sedge, Traveling Sedge, Rush Sedge, Salmon Candy
Latin names: *Banksiola crotchi* (Traveling Sedge) and *Phryganea cinerea* (Rush Sedge)
Size range: #6–12 (15–20 mm, ¾–1 inch)

Key Features

Body: Yellow, brown, or gray; black fringes
Wing cases: Gray to brown; darker than body

Note: Pupal keys for the stillwater caddisflies depend on microscopes. Capture a specimen; note its size, form, and color; and commence firing with an appropriate imitation.

Habitat

Traveling Sedges and related Rush Sedges are most common in stillwaters but also live in a few weedy, slow streams. The Traveling Sedge is best known in the Kamloops region of British Columbia. The Rush Sedge is less well known but is distributed throughout most of the West. There are slight differences in color in these insects, but it's more important to imitate the movement than their exact size and color. Only pupae and adults are important.

Emergence

Pupation begins in spring and takes six to eight weeks. Hatches are in midsummer, primarily in June and July. Traveling Sedge pupae swim to the surface and emerge in open water, in late afternoon or evening. Rush Sedge pupae are reported to swim or crawl across the bottom to shore, where they emerge by crawling out on rushes or sedges, usually at evening, after dark, or at dawn. If you see caddis adults on the water, suspect trout are taking pupae.

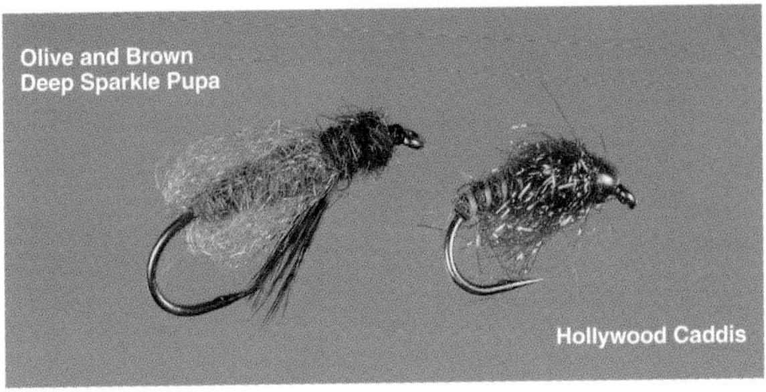

Behavior and Tactics

For Traveling Sedges, which hatch in open water, use a floating line and long leader, or a sinking-tip line, to get your fly to the bottom or near it. Raise the fly with a retrieve in short strips, pausing often to let it rest, as the natural does. For Rush Sedge pupae, use a line that gets your fly to the bottom and keeps it there. Retrieve across the bottom, again with short strips interspersed with pauses. Takes will be hard, and the trout large. Rig with 3X tippets.

Known Hatches

Most of the Kamloops region lakes, and those farther north in BC, have the Traveling Sedge hatch. The Rush Sedge hatch is known as the Salmon Candy in Hosmer Lake, in Oregon, famous for its rare planting of Atlantic salmon.

Traveling Sedge adult

Traveling Sedge adult (Jim Schollmeyer)

Common names: Traveler Sedge, Traveling Sedge, Rush Sedge, Salmon Candy
Latin names: *Banksiola crotchi* (Traveling Sedge) and *Phryganea cinerea* (Rush Sedge)
Size range: #6–12 (15–20 mm, ¾–1 inch)

Key Features

Body: Shades of brown, gray, green, or yellow
Wings: Patterned with gray, brown, or yellow
Antennae: About body length

Habitat

Traveling Sedges and Rush Sedges usually hatch over vegetated shallows, in association with the shoreline, though entomologists report them rising from depths of 100 to 200 feet, so you might encounter them far from shore. They're most important, most often, within a few feet to one hundred feet or so from shore, or over submerged weed beds. The adults are easy to spot motoring on the water, and they're important wherever you see them.

Emergence

Most hatches are in June and July, in afternoon and evening, but they can go on into the night. I've had dawn hatches of Rush Sedges in Oregon that are rarely seen, because nobody else is out there at that time of day. The defining behavior of this group is their scooting on the water. Use imitations that can be skated across the surface. They don't always have to be precisely imitative.

Behavior and Tactics

Traveling Sedge and Rush Sedge adults chug along in the surface film. Trout key on this movement much more than they do on the size, shape, or color of the natural. Even with the emerger pattern, it helps to give it an occasional gentle tug, to set it in motion and send out some waves. It's likely that trout key on the concentric wavelets made by the naturals as much as they do on the insect itself. Scoot them, then rest them. Rig to fish these imitations with stout tippets; takes will not be gentle.

Known Hatches

Traveling Sedges are most famous in the Kamloops region, and many though not all British Columbia lakes. The Rush Sedge is widely distributed but little known. It's likely to be important in many places, but you'll have to be out at dawn or dusk to find them.

15 Midges

Stillwater midge larva

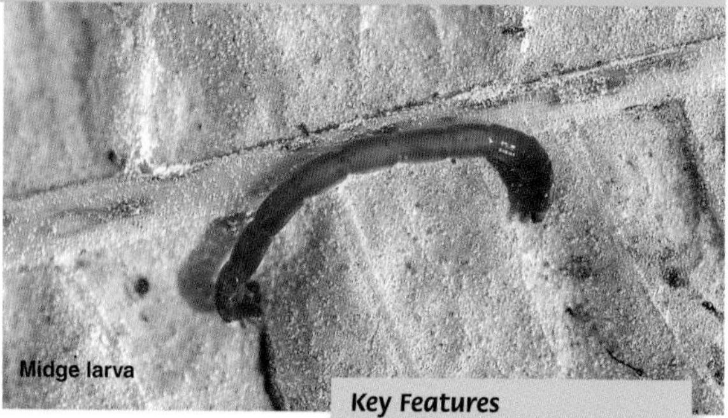

Midge larva

Common names: Midge, chironomid, bloodworm

Latin name: Chironomidae (more than 50 genera and about 1,000 known species)

Size range: #8–22 (5–20 mm, ⅜–¾ inch)

Key Features

Body shape: Wormlike segmented tube

Body color: Red, green, brown, or black

Legs: First and last segments with pair of fleshy prolegs

Head: Small, dark, visible

Habitat

Wormlike midge larvae live in bottom silts and vegetation in lakes and ponds. They are at times carried on gentle wind currents that move through stillwaters. If sunshine strikes into clear water, you can peer into it, and often see midge larvae flick-flicking their bodies aimlessly through the water column. They stand out dramatically, and trout key on them when nothing else is more abundant and available.

Emergence

Midge larvae get loose in the water column most often during spring and fall turnover periods, when lake waters are stirred into a bit of a stew. They also get mixed into the stillwater drift whenever winds become strong and set currents into motion. Trout cruise and feed on whatever they can find; midge larvae are often the most common insect they come across. These trout are not strictly selective, but they don't pass up chances at midge larvae or their imitations.

Behavior and Tactics

Midge larvae flick their bodies back and forth vigorously and then rest. The closest you can come to this behavior is to either suspend an imitation beneath an indicator and let it wind-drift or cast it out on an intermediate or sink-tip line, count it down three or four feet, and then hand-twist retrieve it as slowly as possible. Rig two larvae, or pair a larva pattern with a pupa imitation. The farther north you go, the larger midges get. Fish size 8 to 12 imitations across the northern tier, and size 14 to 20 as you move south.

Known Hatches

Though most famous for the big bloodworms in BC lakes, midge larvae live in every Western pond or lake you'll ever fish. They vary widely across a broad spectrum of sizes and colors. Be sure to observe and imitate those in your own waters.

Stillwater midge pupa

Midge pupa

Common names: Midge, chironomid

Latin name: Chironomidae (more than 50 genera and about 1,000 known species)

Size range: #8–22 (5–20 mm, 3/8–3/4 inch)

Key Features

Body shape: Slender, tapered, distinctly ribbed

Body color: Dark brown, black, red, green

Wing cases: One pair, short, tucked against abdomen

Thorax: Dark; hunchback-like

Gills: Feathery, at top of thorax and end of abdomen, or pair of spiracles on hump

Habitat

Pupation takes place in bottom silts or suspended ooze. Because some midge larvae are able to live at bottom depths where oxygen is absent, trout sometimes feed selectively on them far from shore, over great depths, with no vegetation beds in the area. For the most part, though, these pupae are most important in water depths where sunlight strikes the bottom, from five to twenty-five feet down.

Emergence

Midge pupae suspend just above the bottom and then release to drift and swim to the surface, where they stage again. Trout feed on midge pupae at the two levels: just above the bottom or just beneath the surface. When they're high, you can usually see trout cruising to feed on them. When they're deep, your only hint about it will be the presence of midge adults. Swarms of midges in the air are your clue to fish the bottom with pupa patterns.

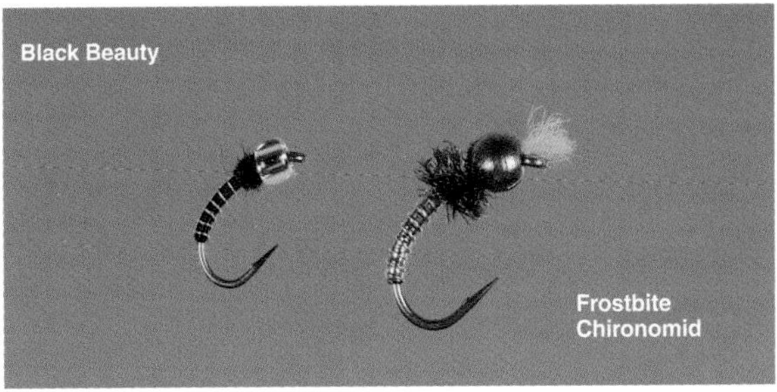

Behavior and Tactics

Trout take most midge pupae when the insects hang vertically, staged above the bottom or beneath the surface. Imitate them at either depth by suspending an imitation, or a pair of them, under an indicator. To fish shallow, drop the patterns one or two feet beneath a small fan of yarn. To fish deep, use a sliding indicator. Measure the depth by clipping your hemostat to the tippet and letting it sink. Then tie an indicator stopper knot eighteen inches short of that depth. Pinch a bit of putty weight between two pupae. They'll slowly sink and suspend. Watch that indicator.

Known Hatches

Be aware of midge pupae on any stillwater you fish. If you have no hint that anything else will work, try measuring the depth and suspending a pair of imitations deep. You'll be surprised at the consistency, and often the size, of the results.

Stillwater midge adult

Midge adult

Common names: Midge, chironomid, buzzer
Latin name: Chironomidae (more than 50 genera and about 1,000 known species)
Size range: #8–22 (5–20 mm, 3/8–3/4 inch)

Key Features

Body shape: Long, slender, tapered
Body color: Brown, black, red, or green
Wings: Single pair, short, held over back
Legs: Long, spindly
Antennae: Males, plumelike tufts

Habitat

Midge adults are important most often around the edges of ponds and lakes, and least often far from shore. On large lakes, they're commonly found in some relation to the shoreline, rarely distant from it, because they need to come to rest at some point in their brief aerial lives. On smaller lakes and ponds, they'll be scattered across the entire surface, because it's all a short flight from shore.

Emergence

Stillwater midges hatch at any season, but I've found the adults most important in early spring and late fall. The farther north you go, the more their importance will be pushed toward summer. In cool weather, midges hatch in the warm part of the day; in warm weather, they emerge at morning and evening. But I've fished consistent emergences of size 22 midge adults at dawn in March and buzzing swarms of egg-depositing adults at dusk throughout the year.

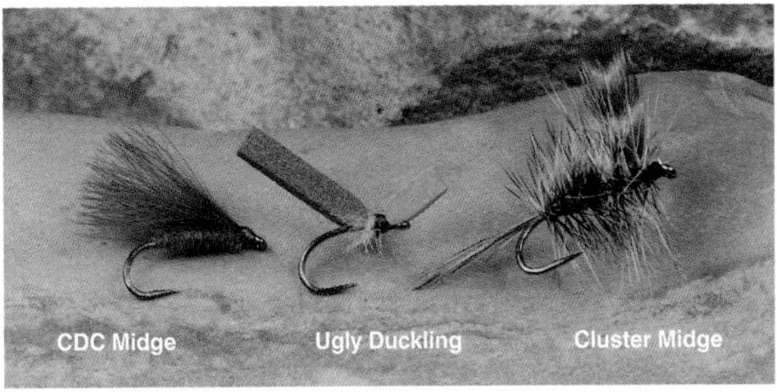

Behavior and Tactics

Midge adults are taken at two primary times: when they emerge through the surface film and when they return to the water to buzz around on the surface, usually just before dark. I use a CDC pattern during emergences and sometimes during egg-laying behavior. The Ugly Duckling seems to work whenever midges are hatching and often when they're not. The cluster pattern can be scooted when the naturals buzz over the surface. Try to pattern a trout's movement, and place the fly where it will rise next. Move the fly a bit and then let it sit.

Known Hatches

The most famous hatches of midges are in the Kamloops, BC, area. Most innovations in midge imitations and fishing come out of that area. Always remember that while northern midges are large, most midges are not, and you might need to downsize patterns for your own waters.

16 Damselflies and Dragonflies

Damselfly nymph

Damselfly nymph

Common names: Damselfly, green damsel
Latin name: Coenagrionidae (and related Lestidae)
Size range: #8–18 (12–25 mm, ½–1 inch)

Key Features

Tails: Three leaf-shaped gills
Body: Long, slender; olive to olive-brown
Wing cases: Visible on mature nymphs
Head: Extensible jaws on underside
Antennae: Visible, short

Habitat

Damselfly nymphs rank in importance alongside *Callibaetis* mayflies and midge pupae. They're hunters among vegetation beds and along the bottom, primarily in lakes and ponds, but also in vegetated backwaters of some moving waters as well. They're almost always found in association with plant beds and will not inhabit open bottoms unless there is enough photosynthetic growth or detrital depositions to attract prey.

Emergence

Damselfly nymphs migrate from offshore plant beds to emerge by crawling out on rushes, reeds, or floating lily pads or duckweed. Migrations usually begin in May and continue through June and July. In northern latitudes and higher elevations, they might be delayed into August. Daily emergence is in afternoon, evening, or after dark. Trout feed on damsel nymphs selectively most often during their migrations, but also take tiny immature nymphs constantly throughout the entire year.

Behavior and Tactics

Damsel nymphs swim with a sinuous side-to-side motion. The best imitations incorporate marabou to mimic this movement. Fish the Baby Damsel at all times of year around plant beds and above the bottom. Rig with a floating or clear intermediate line. Let the fly sink and then retrieve it with the slowest hand-twist. Fish the larger Marabou Damsel in spring and early summer, during migrations, either around vegetation, or just a foot or two deep. Use the same slow retrieve, but insert a few short strips every few feet and then pause to let it sink.

Known Hatches

Kamloops Lks., BC; Chopaka Lk., WA; Crane Prairie Res., OR; Margarita Lk. and Martis Ck. Res., CA; Georgetown Res., MT; Henrys Lk., ID; Yellowstone Lk., WY; Ruby Lks., NV; Strawberry Res., UT; Delaney Butte Lks., CO; Sunrise Lk., AZ; Eagle Nest Lk., NM.

Damselfly adult

Damselfly adult

Common names: Damselfly, blue damsel
Latin name: Coenagrionidae (and related Lestidae)
Size range: #10–12 (25–50 mm, 1–2 inches)

Key Features
Tails: None
Body: Slender, elongated; blue, tan, or red
Wings: Clear, bases narrow; usually held over back
Eyes: Large, separated
Antennae: Very short

Habitat

Adult damselflies fly along the edges of ponds and lakes and over slow-flowing streams with quiet backwaters. They rest on shoreline vegetation, rushes and reeds that protrude from the water, and lily pads and other floating plants. They fly in sunshine and calm air; if clouds cover the sun, or the wind comes up, they immediately go to rest. They mate on the vegetation and in the air.

Emergence

Damselflies begin emerging in May, peak in June and July, and in places continue into August. Nymphs migrate to shore and crawl out on emergent vegetation. The adult escapes the nymphal exoskeleton away from water any time from early afternoon to evening and after dark. At first the adult is pale yellow or olive. Its colors slowly harden into permanent tan, red, or the most common color, blue. After mating, females plant their eggs in submerged reed or lily pad stems.

Behavior and Tactics

Freshly emerged damsels, called *teneral adults,* are often blown to the water and taken by trout. If the wind is strong enough, trout will cruise lake and pond edges and feed on them selectively. Trout feed on mature adults along reed edges and lily pad flats, taking them while they lay their eggs or after they've collapsed to the water. Many adult damsels are also blown to the water by modest to high winds. I've taken trout on both windy and calm days that were crammed with damsel adults, and the trout were obviously selective to them.

Known Hatches

Damselfly adults are important on all of the waters listed in the nymph section. They're also likely to have their moments of importance on any lake or pond you fish during their long spring and summer emergence period.

Dragonfly nymph

Common names: Dragonfly nymph, darner
Latin name: Aeshnidae (and related Libellulidae and Gomphidae)
Size range: #4–12 (25–50 mm, 1–2 inches)

Key Features

Tails: Three short, sharp, protrusions
Body: Hourglass shaped; olive to olive-brown
Wing cases: Visible on mature nymphs
Head: Extensible jaws on underside
Antennae: Short

Habitat

Dragonfly nymphs stalk prey or ambush it in vegetation beds and in woody and leafy debris on the bottom. One family is adapted to moving water, but they're not known to be fed on selectively. Neither are dragonfly adults, though we've all seen trout try to snag them out of the air. Dragonfly nymphs reach their greatest importance in shallow to deep plant beds and over vegetated shoals.

Emergence

Dragonfly nymphs migrate to shore for emergence, along the bottom rather than higher in the water column. This usually happens in June, July, and August. Nymphs crawl out on vegetation for emergence, almost always at dusk or after dark, as a defense against bird predation. They have a two- to four-year life cycle and are fed on by trout before and after a hatch, not just when they're migrating. Fish their imitations whenever you have no hint what else to try.

Behavior and Tactics

Dragonfly nymphs are usually cryptic in the vegetation or along the bottom, but when they are startled by a trout, or when migrating for emergence, they dart along in four- to six-inch bursts. Fish the weighted Beaverpelt on the appropriate line to get it to the bottom. Use a stripping retrieve. The Predator is designed to float above the bottom. Rig it on a three- to four-foot leader and what I call a depth-charge line, one that will plunge right to the bottom. Retrieve it with a few strips and then let it rest. Repeat.

Known Hatches

Dragonfly nymphs are present in nearly all lakes and ponds; the more vegetated the water, the heavier populations you'll find. Always suspect they're present in stillwaters; always give their imitations a try.

17 Water Boatmen

Water boatman adult

Water boatman

Common names: Water boatman, corixid, corixa bug
Latin name: Corixidae
Size range: #10–20 (6–15 mm, ¼–⅝ inch)

Key Features

Body: Beetle-like; olive with black markings
Forewings: Carapaced over back
Legs: Hind legs oarlike

Note: Closely-related back swimmers are usually pale to white; otherwise they are similar.

Habitat

Water boatmen live in all stillwaters and in quiet streams with rooted vegetation. They're most important in shallow plant beds and shoreline vegetation of lakes and ponds and also where vegetation takes root in the slowest parts of some spring creeks and tailwaters. They swim to the surface to take a bubble of air; they're rarely found more than three or four feet deep.

Emergence

Water boatmen grow directly into adults without leaving the water. Mating and egg-laying also take place in the water. They fly only to leave a pond or lake that is drying up or during spring and fall dispersal flights, which can occasionally be heavy enough to cause selective feeding. Because they overwinter as adults, they're most important in late winter and early spring, because they're available to trout then, when many other aquatic insects remain inactive.

Behavior and Tactics

Water boatmen take oxygen from the atmosphere in a bubble held under their wings. They trade back and forth between submerged vegetation and the surface to get a fresh bubble of air. Trout cruise above plant beds, watching for swimming boatmen. The Stillwater Boatman is designed to either suspend beneath a tiny indicator or to float above a tiny split shot. Let it sit; animate it when a trout comes into sight. The Boatman is best fished over vegetation or cast to sighted fish. Place it well ahead, let it sink to the trout's level, and then twitch it.

Known Hatches

Kamloops Lks., BC; Chopaka Lk., WA; Hosmer Lk., OR; Manzanita Lk., CA; Blackfeet Res. Lks., MT; Yellowstone Lk., WY; Otter Ck. Res., UT; Ruby Lks., NV; Henrys Lk., ID; Spinney Mtn. Res., CO; Crescent Lk., AZ; Eagle Nest Lk., NM.

18 Alderflies

Alderfly adult

Alderfly adult

Common names: Alderfly, alder
Latin name: Sialidae
Size range: #10–14
(6–18 mm, ¼–¾ inch)

Key Features
Tails: None
Body: Stout, dark brown to black
Wings: Black, shiny, lack hairs
Thorax: First segment as wide as or wider than head
Antennae: Short, approx. half body length

Habitat

Alderflies are often mistaken for caddisflies, but they have shiny wings, and they're much more blocky. Their larvae live in leaf packs in lakes, ponds, and still eddies and pools of forested streams. Pupation is on land. Only the adult stage is important to anglers. Alderflies are found in heavy enough populations to cause selective feeding in most stillwaters bordered by alders and other trees.

Emergence

Alderflies clamber about in trees beginning with the first warm days of May, peaking in June, and tapering off in July. They fly in the warmth of the sun, from midmorning to late afternoon. When their awkward flights take them over water, they often fall to the surface. Because of their weight, they sink rather than float and are almost always taken by trout beneath the surface. It looks like a dry-fly situation, but you need a wet.

Alderfly

Behavior and Tactics

Alderfly adults are poor fliers and often helicopter into the water. They sink as soon as they begin struggling in the surface film. Trout cruise and watch for them along tree-lined shorelines during warm days of spring and early summer. If a wind comes up, more of them will be blown to the water. If you can cover cruising trout, let your wet imitation simply sink. That's what the naturals do. If you need to cover water to find trout, then cast out, let the Alderfly sink briefly, and retrieve it with slow strips, with intermittent pauses.

Known Hatches

Alderfly hatches are most important on tree-lined lakes and ponds too small to become known. Tie a few of the single pattern to be armed with it when your travels take you to a hidden stillwater where the naturals fall to the water and get eaten by trout.

19 Scuds

Scud

Scuds

Common names: Scud, sideswimmer
Latin name: Amphipoda
Size range: #10–16 (5–20 mm, ⅜–¾ inch)

Key Features

Body shape: Flattened side to side; hardened back
Body color: Light gray to olive or brown
Abdomen: Six segments, each with a pair of swimmer paddles
Thorax: Seven segments, each with a pair of legs
Antennae: Two pairs, about equal in length

Habitat

Scuds are much more important in lakes and ponds than they are in rivers and streams, because their preferred habitat, vegetation beds, is found more often in stillwater than it is in moving water. They're found wherever photosynthetic growth is sufficient for them to feed. They thrive along the shoreline, in shallow coves, in deeper plant beds, and on shoals wherever sunlight strikes and promotes plant growth.

Emergence

Scuds eat, breed, and die without ever leaving the aquatic environment. Their numbers are relatively stable throughout the year, though like trout they're most active when the water is warmer. But they remain important on waters that are open in winter. Imitating them on a stillwater, with at least one nymph in a pair (the other could be a midge pupa) is a good idea whenever you're on a lake or pond and no specific insect is hatching to attract trout.

Behavior and Tactics

Scuds keep busy, swimming from place to place in vegetation, seemingly without direction. The key to fishing them is selecting a line with the right sink rate to get imitations to the level of vegetation. It's wise to use a slow hand-twist retrieve to keep the nymph deep as long as possible. Don't overlook the Shellback Scuds listed in the moving water section; they'll work as well in lakes. The Beadhead Scud represents a female carrying eggs. The Fast-Sinking Scud is useful for getting quickly down to visible, cruising trout in lakes with clear water.

Known Hatches

Few lakes and ponds lack scuds. To list famous hatches would detract from their importance on all Western stillwaters, where you should always be prepared to imitate them.

20

Leeches

Leech

Common names: Leech, bloodsucker
Latin name: Hirudinea
Size range: #4–14 (12–75 mm, ½–3 inches)

Key Features

Body shape: Foreshortened and flattened or elongated and wormlike; sucker at each end
Body color: Tan, olive, reddish brown, black; plain or speckled

Habitat

Leeches live in streams and stillwaters, but they're most important in lakes and ponds. They feed on decaying organic material and are most abundant where dead vegetative and animal matter settles to the bottom. They thrive in shallow coves with lush growth but can be found in most stillwater environments, from shoreline waters to the dark depths of marl-laden lakes.

Emergence

Leeches have no emergence period. They're important any time of year; if a stillwater is open to trout fishing, a leech imitation will be a reasonable choice if no other food form is evident and active. Though leeches get very large, sometimes four inches long, trout for some reason seem not to feed on the biggest of them. Most leeches I've found in throat and stomach samples are an inch to an inch-and-a-half long, rarely two inches.

Behavior and Tactics

Black patterns are shown here just as samples. Dark olive and reddish brown are just as common. Leeches usually creep along, but at times swim boldly in open water with a snakelike motion. Fish imitations on the sink, on a slow hand-twist, and alternate with a stripping retrieve. It's not uncommon to see small leeches, half an inch to an inch long, hanging from the surface of a lake in spring and summer. Trout pluck them gently. I tie my leeches in small sizes, 10 to 14, and often pinch half the tails and hackles off my Woolly Buggers before fishing them.

Known Hatches

Leeches inhabit almost all lakes and ponds. An imitation makes an excellent choice on all stillwaters. When trolling, I'll use a leech pattern paired with a smaller scud or midge dressing as a trailer. It's an excellent way to explore for trout.

PART FOUR

Fly Pattern Dressings

21 Patterns for Moving Water Hatches

Mayflies

Blue-Winged Olive nymph

Pheasant Tail Flashback

(originator: Frank Sawyer)

Hook:	#16–22, 1XL nymph
Thread:	Brown 8/0
Tail:	Pheasant tail fibers
Rib:	Copper wire, counterwound
Abdomen:	Pheasant tail fibers
Wing case:	Pearl Flashabou
Thorax:	Peacock herl
Legs:	Pheasant tail fiber tips

Baetis Nymph

Hook:	#16–22, 1XL nymph
Weight:	8–12 turns non-lead wire
Thread:	Olive 8/0
Tails:	Olive-dyed mallard flank
Abdomen:	Olive rabbit dubbing
Wing case:	Mottled turkey section
Thorax:	Brown dubbing

Blue-Winged Olive dun

Olive Sparkle Dun

(originator: Craig Mathews)

Hook:	#16–22 dry fly
Thread:	Olive 8/0
Wing:	Natural compara-dun deer hair
Shuck:	Olive-brown Z-Lon
Body:	Olive rabbit dubbing

BWO Parachute

Hook:	#16–22 dry fly
Thread:	Olive 8/0
Wing post:	Light gray turkey flat
Tail:	Blue dun hackle fibers, split
Body:	Olive synthetic dubbing
Hackle:	Blue dun

Blue-Winged Olive spinner

Red Quill Spinner

Hook:	#16–22 dry fly
Thread:	Brown 8/0
Tails:	Brown hackle fibers, split
Body:	Red-dyed hackle stem
Wings:	Light dun hen hackle tips, spent
Hackle:	Brown, clipped top and bottom

Blue Quill Spinner

Hook:	#16–22 dry fly
Thread:	Gray 8/0
Tails:	Blue dun hackle fibers, split
Body:	Blue-dyed hackle stem
Wings:	Light dun hen hackle tips, spent
Hackle:	Blue dun, clipped top and bottom

Brown Dun

Brown Compara-dun

(orginators: Al Caucci and Bob Nastasi)
Hook: #12–14 dry fly
Thread: Brown 6/0 or 8/0
Wing: Brown compara-dun deer hair
Tail: Brown hackle fibers, split
Body: Olive-brown synthetic dubbing

Gray Drake nymph

Near Enough

(originator: Polly Rosborough)
Hook: #10–12, 3XL nymph
Thread: Gray 3/0 or 6/0
Tail: Barred mallard flank
Body: Light gray fox underfur
Legs: Barred mallard flank
Wing case: Butts of leg fibers

Gray Drake spinner

Black Drake Spinner

(modified from Polly Rosborough)
Hook: #10–12 dry fly
Tread: Black 6/0
Tail: Dark blue dun hackle fibers, split
Hackle: Dark blue dun, clipped on bottom
Body: Red-brown synthetic dubbing

Pale Morning Dun nymph

Beadhead Fox Squirrel

(originator: Dave Whitlock)
Hook: #14–18, 1XL nymph
Head: Gold bead

Weight: 8–12 turns non-lead wire
Thread: Brown 6/0
Tail: Red fox or pine squirrel guard hairs
Body: Red fox or pine squirrel underfur
Thorax: Red fox or pine squirrel fur, with guard hairs

Beadhead PMD Nymph

(originator: Rick Hafele)
Hook: #14–18, 1X short curved scud
Head: Gold bead
Weight: 6–8 turns non-lead wire
Thread: Brown 8/0
Tail: Ginger hackle fibers
Rib: Copper wire
Abdomen: Cinnamon fur dubbing
Thorax: Red fox or pine squirrel fur, with guard hairs

Pale Morning Dun

PMD Sparkle Dun

(originator: Craig Mathews)
Hook: #16–18 dry fly
Thread: Tan 8/0
Wing: Light compara-dun deer hair
Tail: Brown Z-Lon
Body: Pale yellow-olive synthetic dubbing

PMD Thorax Dun

(originator: Mike Lawson)
Hook: #16–18 dry fly
Thread: Tan 8/0
Wing: Light gray turkey flat
Tail: Light ginger hackle fibers, splayed
Body: Pale yellow-olive synthetic dubbing
Hackle: Light ginger, fore and aft of wing, clipped on bottom

Pale Morning Dun spinner

Ginger Quill Spinner

Hook:	#16–18 dry fly
Thread:	Tan 8/0
Tails:	Ginger hackle fibers, split
Body:	Ginger-dyed hackle stem
Wings:	Light blue dun hen hackle tips, spent
Hackle:	Ginger, clipped top and bottom

Lesser Green Drake nymph

Beadhead Hare's Ear

Hook:	#12–14, 1XL nymph
Head:	Gold bead
Weight:	10–12 turns non-lead wire
Thread:	Brown 6/0 or 8/0
Tail:	Hare's mask guard hairs
Abdomen:	Hare's mask fur
Thorax:	Dark hare's mask fur, with guard hairs

Flav Nymph

Hook:	#12–14, 1XL nymph
Weight:	10–15 turns non-lead wire
Thread:	Brown 6/0 or 8/0
Tail:	Brown partridge fibers
Body:	Light brown fur dubbing
Wing case:	Mottled turkey feather section
Thorax:	Dark brown fur dubbing
Legs:	Brown partridge fibers

Lesser Green Drake dun

Olive Quigley Cripple

(originator: Bob Quigley)

Hook:	#12–14 dry fly
Thread:	Brown 6/0 or 8/0

Tail:	Olive marabou fluff
Abdomen:	Olive rabbit dubbing
Thorax:	Peacock herl
Wing:	Deer hair, tips forward, butts clipped
Hackle:	Olive-dyed grizzly

Frying Pan Biot Green Drake Dun

(originator: A. K. Best)

Hook:	#12–14 dry fly
Thread:	Olive 6/0 or 8/0
Tail:	Moose body hair, splayed
Body:	Green-dyed turkey biot
Wings:	Medium blue dun hen hackle tips
Hackle:	Blue dun and olive-dyed grizzly, mixed

Lesser Green Drake spinner

CDC Rusty Spinner

(originator: René Harrop)

Hook:	#12–14 dry fly
Thread:	Brown 6/0 or 8/0
Tails:	Light blue dun hackle fibers, split
Abdomen:	Rusty-brown goose biot
Wings:	White CDC topped with gray Z-Lon
Thorax:	Rusty brown dubbing

Western Green Drake nymph

Gold-Ribbed Hare's Ear

Hook:	#8–12, 1XL nymph
Weight:	10–20 turns non-lead wire
Thread:	Brown 6/0
Tail:	Hare's mask guard hairs
Rib:	Oval gold tinsel
Abdomen:	Hare's mask fur
Wing case:	Mottled turkey feather section
Thorax and legs:	Dark hare's mask, with guard hairs

Western Green Drake Nymph

Hook:	#8–12, 2XL nymph
Weight:	10–20 turns non-lead wire
Thread:	Brown 6/0 or 8/0
Tails:	Brown partridge fibers
Rib:	Gold wire
Abdomen:	Brown rabbit dubbing
Wing case:	Black goose feather section
Thorax:	Brown rabbit fur and Antron, mixed, teased out for legs

Western Green Drake dun

Green Drake Quigley Cripple

(originator: Bob Quigley)

Hook:	#8–12 dry fly
Thread:	Olive 6/0
Tail:	Olive-dyed grizzly marabou fluff
Rib:	Yellow floss
Abdomen:	Olive rabbit dubbing
Thorax:	Peacock herl
Wing:	Deer hair, tips forward, butts short
Hackle:	Olive-dyed grizzly

Green Paradrake

(originator: Mike Lawson)

Hook:	#10–12 dry fly
Thread:	Yellow 3/0
Wing post:	Dark gray elk hair
Tail:	Three moose body hairs
Body:	Olive-dyed elk hair, extended
Hackle:	Grizzly dyed yellow, parachute

Western Green Drake spinner

Red Quill Spinner

Hook: #10–12 dry fly
Thread: Brown 6/0
Tails: Brown hackle fibers, split
Body: Dyed red quill hackle stem
Wings: Light blue dun hen hackle tips
Hackle: Brown, clipped top and bottom
Thorax: Rusty dubbing

Green Drake Spinner

(originator: Sylvester Nemes)
Hook: #10–12 dry fly
Thread: Olive 6/0
Tails: Three golden pheasant crest fibers
Rib: Fine gold wire
Abdomen: Dark green floss
Thorax: Dark brown dubbing
Wings: Off-white hackle, wound and drawn to sides

Great Red Quill dun

Timpanoga Quigley Cripple

(originator: Bob Quigley)
Hook: #8–12 standard dry
Thread: Olive
Tails: Olive-brown marabou fluff
Rib: Yellow floss
Abdomen: Olive-brown synthetic dubbing
Thorax: Peacock herl
Wing: Deer hair, tips forward, butts clipped
Hackle: Grizzly dyed olive-brown

Blue-Winged Red Quill

Hook:	#8–12 standard dry
Thread:	Brown 6/0
Wings:	Dun-dyed deer hair
Tail:	Moose body hair
Body:	Rust and olive synthetic dubbing, mixed
Hackle:	Dark blue dun

Small Blue-Winged Olive Nymph

Pheasant Tail

(originator: Al Troth)

Hook:	#16–18 standard nymph, 1XL
Thread:	Brown 8/0
Tails:	Pheasant tail fibers
Rib:	Fine copper wire
Body:	Pheasant tail fibers
Wing case:	Pheasant tail fibers
Thorax:	Peacock herl
Legs:	Tips of wing case fibers

Margarita Fur Nymph

(originators: John Juracek and Craig Mathews)

Hook:	#16–18 standard nymph, 1XL
Thread:	Brown 8/0
Tails:	Brown partridge fibers
Body:	Dark brown rabbit dubbing
Legs:	Picked-out rabbit dubbing

Small Blue-Winged Olive Dun

Olive Sparkle Dun

(originator: Craig Mathews)

Hook:	#16–18 standard dry
Thread:	Olive 8/0
Wing:	Dun-dyed deer hair

Shuck: Amber Z-Lon
Body: Olive rabbit dubbing

Olive Thorax Dun

Hook: #16–18 standard dry
Thread: Olive 8/0
Wing post: Light gray turkey flat
Tail: Dun hackle fibers, splayed
Body: Olive synthetic dubbing
Hackle: Light dun, clipped on bottom

Mahogany dun

Mahogany Sparkle Dun

Hook: #12–18 standard dry
Thread: Brown 8/0
Wing: Natural brown compara-dun deer hair
Shuck: Amber Z-Lon
Body: Brown rabbit dubbing

Mahogany Thorax Dun

Hook: #12–18 standard dry
Thread: Brown 8/0
Wing: Gray turkey flat
Tails: Brown hackle fibers, split
Body: Brown synthetic dubbing
Hackle: Dark blue dun, clipped on bottom

Mahogany spinner

Red Quill Spinner

Hook: #12–18 standard dry
Thread: Brown 8/0
Tails: Brown hackle fibers, split
Body: Dyed red-quill hackle stem
Wings: White hen hackle tips, spent
Hackle: Brown, clipped top and bottom

Blue Quill Spinner

Hook:	#12–18 standard dry
Thread:	Gray 8/0
Tails:	Light blue dun hackle fibers, split
Body:	Peacock herl, stripped
Wings:	White hen hackle tips, spent
Hackle:	Light blue dun, clipped on bottom

Trico dun

Trico Female Sparkle Dun

Hook:	#18–24 standard dry
Thread:	Olive 8/0
Wing:	Pale compara-dun deer hair
Shuck:	Amber Z-Lon
Body:	Pale olive fur dubbing

Trico Male No-Hackle Dun

Hook:	#18–24 standard dry
Thread:	Brown 8/0
Tails:	Light blue dun hackle fibers, split
Body:	Brown synthetic dubbing
Wings:	Light mallard or teal wing segments
Head:	Black synthetic dubbing

Trico spinner

Soft-Hackle Trico Spinner

(originator: Rick Hafele)

Hook:	#18–22, 1X heavy wet fly
Thread:	Gray 8/0
Tail:	Blue dun hackle fibers
Body:	Muskrat fur
Hackle:	Blue dun hen, sparse

Female Trico Poly-Wing Spinner

Hook:	#18–24 standard dry
Thread:	Brown 8/0
Tails:	Gray Microfibetts, split
Abdomen:	Olive rabbit dubbing with black egg sac
Wings:	White polypro yarn
Thorax:	Brown rabbit dubbing

Male Trico Poly-Wing Spinner

Hook:	#18–24 standard dry
Thread:	Black 8/0
Tails:	Gray Microfibetts, split
Abdomen:	Black synthetic dubbing
Wings:	White polypro yarn
Thorax:	Black rabbit dubbing

Western March Brown nymph

Pheasant Tail

(originator: Frank Sawyer)

Hook:	#12–16, 1XL nymph
Weight:	10–15 turns non-lead wire
Thread:	Brown 8/0
Tail:	Pheasant tail fibers
Rib:	Copper wire, counterwound
Body:	Pheasant tail fibers as herl
Wing case:	Pheasant tail fibers
Thorax:	Peacock herl
Legs:	Wing case tips

March Brown Spider

(originator: Sylvester Nemes)

Hook:	#12–16, 2X heavy wet fly
Thread:	Orange silk or 6/0
Rib:	Oval gold tinsel
Body:	Hare's mask fur
Hackle:	Brown partridge

Western March Brown duns

March Brown Compara-dun

(originators: Al Caucci and Bob Nastasi)

Hook:	#12–16 standard dry
Thread:	Tan 6/0 or 8/0
Wing:	Natural tan compara-dun deer hair
Tails:	White Microfibetts, split
Body:	Tan synthetic dubbing

March Brown Parachute

(originator: Bob Borden)

Hook:	#12–16 standard dry
Thread:	Tan 6/0 or 8/0
Wing post:	Natural brown deer hair
Tail:	Brown hackle fibers, split
Body:	Hareline Dubbin' Hare's Mask #4
Hackle:	Brown, parachute

Pale Evening Dun

Light Cahill Wet

Hook:	#12–16, 2X heavy wet
Thread:	Tan 8/0
Tails:	Light ginger hackle fibers
Body:	Cream rabbit dubbing
Hackle:	Light ginger hen
Wing:	Wood duck flank

Pale Evening Thorax Dun

Hook:	#12–16 standard dry
Thread:	Tan 8/0
Wing:	White turkey flat
Tails:	Ginger hackle fibers, split
Body:	Cream rabbit dubbing
Hackle:	Ginger

Pale Evening Dun spinner

Western Ginger Quill Spinner

(originator: Fred Arbona Jr.)

Hook:	#12–16 standard dry
Thread:	Tan 8/0
Tails:	Ginger hackle fibers, split
Body:	Pale cream rabbit dubbing
Wings:	Light dun hen feather tips
Hackle:	Ginger, clipped top and bottom

Brown Drake dun

Brown Paradrake

(originator: Mike Lawson)

Hook:	#12 standard dry
Thread:	Brown 3/0
Wing post:	Brown deer hair
Hackle:	Grizzly dyed brown, parachute
Tails:	Three moose body hairs
Body:	Yellowish-tan dyed elk hair, extended

Stoneflies

Little Brown Stone adult

Little Brown Stone

(originator: Polly Rosborough)

Hook:	#14–18, 2XL
Thread:	Brown 8/0
Tail:	Pheasant tail fibers
Body:	Dark brown synthetic dubbing
Wing:	Grizzly hackle tips
Hackle:	Grizzly

Little Brown Buzzer

(originator: Dave Hughes)
Hook: #14–18, 2XL
Thread: Brown 8/0
Egg ball: White polypro yarn
Tails: Pheasant tail fibers, split
Body: Brown synthetic dubbing
Hackle: Grizzly, V notch clipped in bottom

Olive Sally adult

Partridge & Green

(originator: Sylvester Nemes)
Hook: #14–18, 2X heavy wet fly
Thread: Green silk or 6/0
Hackle: Gray partridge
Body: Green silk thread or floss
Thorax: Hare's mask fur

Olive Sally

Hook: #14–18, 2XL
Thread: Olive 8/0
Egg sac: Red dubbing
Tails: Dyed green pheasant tail fibers, split
Body: Pale olive synthetic dubbing
Wings: Light blue dun hackle tips
Hackle: Light blue dun

Yellow Sally nymph

Copper John

(originator: John Barr)
Hook: #12–16, 2XL
Head: Gold bead
Weight: 8–12 turns non-lead wire
Thread: Black 8/0

Tails: Tan goose biots, forked
Abdomen: Copper wire
Wing case: Pearl Flashabou over black Thin Skin, epoxied
Thorax: Peacock herl
Legs: Brown hen back fibers

Yellow Sally Nymph

Hook: #12–16, 3XL
Head: Gold bead
Weight: 8–12 turns non-lead wire
Thread: Tan 8/0
Tail: Tan goose biots, forked
Rib: Copper wire
Abdomen: Tan rabbit dubbing
Wing case: Turkey tail feather section
Thorax: Tan rabbit dubbing, picked out for legs

Yellow Sally adult

Light Cahill Wet

Hook: #12–16, 2X heavy
Thread: Tan 8/0
Tail: Ginger hackle fibers
Body: Cream Light Cahill rabbit fur dubbing
Hackle: Ginger hen
Wing: Wood duck flank fibers

Yellow Sally

Hook: #12–16, 2XL
Thread: Tan 8/0
Egg sac: Amber dubbing
Tails: Pheasant tail fibers, split
Body: Creamish tan synthetic dubbing
Wings: Ginger hackle tips
Hackle: Ginger

Skwala nymph

Skwala Nymph

Hook:	#10–12, 3XL
Head:	Gold bead
Weight:	10–15 turns non-lead wire
Thread:	Brown 3/0 or 6/0
Tails:	Ginger biots, forked
Rib:	Copper wire
Body:	Brown-amber rabbit dubbing
Wing case:	Mottled turkey feather section
Thorax:	Brown-amber rabbit dubbing
Legs:	Ginger hen hackle fibers

Skwala adult

Skwala Egg-Layer

Hook:	#10–12, 2XL or 3XL
Thread:	Brown 3/0 or 6/0
Egg sac:	Black foam
Tails:	Ginger biots, forked
Rib:	Working thread
Body:	Golden-amber synthetic dubbing
Wing:	Brown bucktail
Hackle:	Grizzly and ginger mixed, clipped in V notch

Golden Stonefly nymph

Golden Stone Nymph

Hook:	#6–12, 3XL
Head:	Gold tungsten bead
Weight:	15–20 turns non-lead wire
Thread:	Brown 3/0 or 6/0
Tails:	Ginger biots, forked
Rib:	Amber D rib
Abdomen and thorax:	Golden-brown rabbit fur and Antron, mixed
Wing case:	Mottled dark turkey feather section
Legs:	Ginger hen hackle

Golden Stonefly adult

Stimulator

(originator: Randall Kaufmann)

Hook:	#6–12, 3XL
Thread:	Orange 3/0 or 6/0
Tail:	Natural elk hair
Rib:	Brown hackle, palmered over abdomen
Abdomen:	Golden-brown rabbit dubbing
Wing:	Natural elk hair
Thorax:	Amber synthetic dubbing
Hackle:	Grizzly, palmered over thorax

Warren's Golden Stonefly

(originator: Gary Warren)

Hook:	#6–8 standard dry
Thread:	Brown 6/0
Body:	Golden-tan foam, extended
Wing:	Deer hair
Legs:	Brown rubber legs
Thorax:	Yellow-brown synthetic dubbing

Salmonfly nymph

Montana Stone

(originator: Charles Brooks)

Hook:	#4–8, 3XL
Weight:	20–30 turns non-lead wire
Thread:	Black 3/0
Tail:	Black biots, forked
Rib:	Amber D rib
Body:	Black yarn or fur dubbing
Gills:	White ostrich herl
Hackle:	One grizzly and one brown-dyed grizzly

Salmonfly Simplicity

(originator: Dave Hughes)

Hook:	#6–12, 3XL
Head:	Black tungsten bead
Weight:	15–20 turns non-lead wire
Thread:	Black 3/0 or 6/0
Tails:	Black biots, forked
Rib:	Copper wire
Body:	Black rabbit dubbing, mixed with Antron
Gills:	White ostrich herl
Legs:	Black rubber legs
Thorax:	Black rabbit dubbing, mixed with Antron

Salmonfly adult

Improved Sofa Pillow

(originator: Pat Barnes)

Hook:	#4–8, 3XL
Thread:	Black 6/0
Tail:	Natural elk hair
Rib:	Undersized brown hackle
Body:	Orange yarn or rabbit fur dubbing
Wing:	Natural elk hair
Hackle:	Brown

Warren's Salmonfly

(originator: Gary Warren)

Hook:	#6–10 standard dry
Thread:	Orange 6/0
Body:	Orange foam, extended, colored with brown waterproof pen
Wing:	Yearling elk hair
Legs:	Brown rubber legs
Thorax:	Dark brown synthetic dubbing

Caddisflies

Spotted Sedge larva

Tan Caddis Larva

Hook:	#10–16 curved scud
Head:	Brass bead
Weight:	10–15 turns non-lead wire
Thread:	Brown 6/0 or 8/0
Rib:	Amber D rib
Abdomen:	Tan rabbit dubbing
Thorax:	Pine squirrel fur, with guard hairs

Olive Caddis Larva

Hook:	#10–16 curved scud
Head:	Brass bead
Weight:	10–15 turns non-lead wire
Thread:	Brown 6/0 or 8/0
Rib:	Yellow floss
Abdomen:	Caddis green rabbit dubbing
Thorax:	Pine squirrel fur, with guard hairs

Spotted Sedge pupa

Deep Sparkle Pupa

(originator: Gary LaFontaine)

Hook:	#12–16, 1XL nymph
Weight:	12–15 turns non-lead wire
Thread:	Olive or tan 8/0
Overbody:	Olive or tan sparkle yarn
Underbody:	Olive or tan Touch Dubbing
Legs and antennae:	Brown partridge fibers
Head:	Brown rabbit and Antron, mixed

Beadhead Caddis Pupa

Hook:	#10–16 curved scud
Head:	Brass bead
Weight:	10–15 turns non-lead wire
Thread:	Olive or tan 8/0
Abdomen:	Olive or tan rabbit dubbing
Thorax and wing cases:	Brown rabbit and Antron, mixed, picked out to sides

Spotted Sedge adult

Emergent Sparkle Pupa

(originator: Gary LaFontaine)

Hook:	#10–16 standard dry
Thread:	Tan 8/0
Overbody:	Tan sparkle yarn
Underbody:	Olive Touch Dubbing
Wing:	Natural deer hair
Head:	Brown dubbing

Elk Hair Caddis

(originator: Al Troth)

Hook:	#10–16 standard dry
Thread:	Tan 6/0 or 8/0
Hackle:	Ginger, palmered over body
Body:	Tan rabbit dubbing
Wing:	Elk body hair

Little Sister Sedge larva

Pale Caddis Larva

Hook:	#14–18 curved scud
Head:	Brass bead
Weight:	8–12 turns non-lead wire
Thread:	Brown 6/0 or 8/0
Abdomen:	Pale olive rabbit dubbing
Thorax:	Brown rabbit and Antron, mixed

Little Sister Sedge Pupa

Hook:	#14–18 curved scud
Weight:	8–12 turns non-lead wire
Thread:	Brown 8/0
Abdomen:	Pale green rabbit dubbing
Thorax:	Pine squirrel fur

Partridge & Green

(originator: Sylvester Nemes)

Hook:	#14–18, 1X heavy wet
Thread:	Olive silk or 8/0
Body:	Olive silk or floss
Thorax:	Hare's mask fur
Hackle:	Gray partridge

Olive X-Caddis

(originators: Juracek and Mathews)

Hook:	#16–20 standard dry
Thread:	Olive 8/0
Shuck:	Gray Z-Lon
Body:	Pale olive rabbit dubbing
Wing:	Natural deer hair

Olive Elk Hair Caddis

Hook:	#14–20 standard dry
Thread:	Olive 8/0
Hackle:	Light dun, palmered
Body:	Pale olive rabbit dubbing
Wing:	Light tan deer hair

Gray Sedge adult

Deer Hair Caddis

(originator: Jim Schollmeyer)

Hook:	#10–14 standard dry
Thread:	Brown 6/0
Hackle:	Dark dun, palmered, clipped on bottom
Body:	Olive synthetic dubbing
Wing:	Natural gray deer hair

Leadwing Coachman

Hook:	#12–14 standard wet
Thread:	Black 6/0 or 8/0
Hackle:	Furnace hen
Tag and rib:	Silver Mylar tinsel
Body:	Peacock herl
Wing:	Mallard wing feather sections

Little Black Short-Horned Sedge larva

Cream Midge Nymph

(originator: Ed Koch)

Hook:	#16–20 curved scud
Weight:	8–12 turns non-lead wire
Thread:	Tan 8/0
Rib:	Copper wire
Body:	Cream rabbit dubbing

Maggoty

(originator: Dave Hughes)

Hook:	#16–20 curved scud
Bead:	Black tungsten
Weight:	8–10 turns non-lead wire
Thread:	Black 8/0
Abdomen:	Cream rabbit dubbing
Thorax:	Peacock herl

Little Black Short-Horned Sedge pupa

Cream Caddis Pupa

Hook:	#16–20 curved scud
Head:	Gold bead
Weight:	8–12 turns non-lead wire
Thread:	Tan 8/0
Body:	Cream rabbit dubbing
Thorax:	Brown rabbit and Antron, mixed, picked out

Tan Deep Sparkle Pupa

(originator: Gary LaFontaine)

Hook:	#16–20, 1X heavy wet
Weight:	10–12 turns non-lead wire
Thread:	Tan 8/0
Overbody:	Tan sparkle yarn
Underbody:	Cream Touch Dubbing
Legs and antennae:	Brown partridge fibers
Head:	Brown rabbit and Antron, mixed

Little Black Short-Horned Sedge adult

Deer Hair Caddis

(originator: Jim Schollmeyer)

Hook:	#16–20 standard dry
Thread:	Gray 8/0
Hackle:	Dark blue dun, palmered, clipped
Body:	Dark olive synthetic dubbing
Wing:	Natural gray deer hair

Starling & Herl

Hook:	#16–20, 1X heavy wet
Thread:	Black 8/0
Body:	Peacock herl
Hackle:	Starling

American Grannom larva

Herl Nymph

Hook:	#12–16, 2XL
Weight:	10–15 turns non-lead wire
Thread:	Black 8/0
Body:	Peacock herl
Legs:	Black hackle fibers
Head:	Black ostrich herl

Herl Cased-Caddis Larva

Hook:	#12–16, 2XL
Head:	Gold bead
Weight:	10–15 turns non-lead wire
Thread:	Black 8/0
Body:	Peacock herl
Neck:	Green rabbit dubbing
Legs:	Black hen hackle, clipped on top and bottom

American Grannom pupa

Mother's Day Caddis

(originator: Sylvester Nemes)

Hook:	#12–16, 1X heavy wet
Thread:	Black 8/0
Rib:	Single strand yellow floss
Body:	Peacock herl
Hackle:	One turn brown partridge, gathered on top
Head:	Mole fur

Wired Pupa

(originator: Dave Hughes)

Hook:	#14–18, 1XL nymph
Head:	Black tungsten bead
Thread:	Black 8/0
Body:	Chartreuse Ultra Wire
Thorax:	Pine squirrel fur

American Grannom adult

Black Snowshoe Caddis

(originator: Jim Schollmeyer)

Hook:	#14–18 standard dry
Thread:	Black 8/0
Body:	Black synthetic dubbing
Wing:	Black snowshoe foot hair

Little Caddis Thing

(originator: Tracy Peterson)

Hook:	#14–18 standard dry
Thread:	Gray 8/0
Abdomen:	CDC feather, twisted and wound
Wing:	Four natural gray CDC feather tips
Thorax:	Pine squirrel fur
Antennae:	Pheasant tail fibers

Little Western Weedy-Water Sedge pupa

Little Wired Pupa

(originator: Dave Hughes)

Hook:	#16–20, 1X heavy wet
Head:	Gold bead
Thread:	Brown 8/0
Body:	Chartreuse wire
Thorax:	Brown rabbit and Antron, mixed, picked out

Olive Deep Sparkle Pupa

(originator: Gary LaFontaine)

Hook:	#16–20, 1X heavy wet
Thread:	Brown 8/0
Overbody:	Gray Sparkle Yarn
Underbody:	Olive Touch Dubbing
Legs and antennae:	Black hen hackle fibers
Thorax:	Brown rabbit and Antron, mixed

Little Western Weedy-Water Sedge adult

Deer Hair Caddis

(originator: Jim Schollmeyer)

Hook:	#16–22 standard dry
Thread:	Olive 8/0
Hackle:	Dark blue dun, palmered, clipped on bottom
Body:	Dark olive synthetic dubbing
Wing:	Natural gray deer hair

Olive CDC Caddis

Hook:	#16–22 standard dry
Thread:	Black 8/0
Body:	Dark green synthetic dubbing
Wing:	Natural gray CDC

Long-Horned Sedge adult

Ginger Emergent Sparkle Pupa

(originator: Gary LaFontaine)

Hook:	#14–18 standard dry
Thread:	Tan 8/0
Overbody:	Tan Sparkle Yarn
Underbody:	Tan Touch Dubbing
Wing:	Natural pale deer hair
Head:	Tan dubbing

Ginger Spent Caddis

Hook:	#14–18 standard dry
Thread:	Tan 8/0
Abdomen:	Cream rabbit dubbing
Wings:	Ginger hackle tips
Hackle:	Ginger, over thorax, clipped on bottom and top
Thorax:	Tan rabbit dubbing

Fall Caddis larva

Fall Caddis Larva

Hook:	#6–12, 3XL
Weight:	15–20 turns non-lead wire
Thread:	Black 6/0
Rib:	Amber D rib
Body:	Cream-yellow rabbit dubbing
Legs:	Black hen hackle fibers
Head:	Black ostrich herl

Fall Caddis pupa

Brick Back Caddis

(originator: Skip Morris)

Hook:	#6–10, 2XL curved shank
Head:	Black bead
Weight:	15–20 turns non-lead wire
Thread:	Brown 6/0 or 8/0
Back:	Brown poly yarn overwound with body dubbing
Abdomen:	Amber Sparkle Nymph dubbing
Hackle:	Brown hen back
Thorax:	Brown Sparkle Nymph dubbing

Fall Caddis adult

Orange Bucktail Caddis

Hook:	#6–12 standard dry
Thread:	Orange 6/0
Hackle:	Brown, palmered
Body:	Orange rabbit dubbing
Wing:	Natural brown deer hair

Fall Caddis

Hook:	#6–12 standard dry
Thread:	Brown 6/0
Rib hackle:	Brown, undersized
Body:	Orange dubbing
Wing:	Natural brown deer hair
Hackle:	Brown

McKenzie Caddis larva

Czech Nymph

Hook:	#8–12 curved scud
Head:	Black tungsten bead
Weight:	15–25 turns non-lead wire
Thread:	Black 6/0
Overrib:	3X monofilament
Shellback:	Black Thin Skin
Body rib:	Flat gold tinsel
Body:	Brown dubbing/green fur/brown dubbing

McKenzie Caddis pupa

Olive Soft Hackle

Hook:	#8–12 standard wet fly
Thread:	Olive 6/0
Body:	Green chenille
Hackle:	Gray partridge or pheasant rump

Olive Tied-Down Caddis

Hook:	#8–12 standard wet fly
Thread:	Olive 6/0
Rib:	Ginger hackle, palmered over body
Body:	Green floss
Wing:	Brown bucktail, tied down at end of body
Hackle:	Ginger

McKenzie Caddis adult

Great Gray Sedge

Hook: #6–10 standard dry
Thread: Olive 6/0
Hackle: Medium blue dun, palmered
Body: Dark olive synthetic dubbing
Wing: Gray-dyed yearling elk

CDC Elk Hair Olive

(originator: Brian Marz)
Hook: #10 standard dry
Thread: Olive 6/0
Body: Olive synthetic dubbing
Hackle: Olive CDC, palmered
Wing: Gray-dyed yearling elk

Midges and crane flies

Midge pupa

Syl's Midge

(originator: Sylvester Nemes)
Hook: #16–18 standard dry
Thread: Olive 8/0
Body: Peacock herl
Hackle: Gray partridge, one turn

Thread Midge

(originator: Gary Wilmuth)
Hook: #18–24 curved scud
Thread: Black 6/0 or 8/0
Rib: Working thread
Abdomen: White, red, or green 6/0 or 8/0 thread
Thorax: Lump of working thread

Midge adult

Griffith's Gnat

(originator: George Griffith)

Hook:	#16–24 standard dry
Thread:	Black 8/0 or 10/0
Body:	Peacock herl
Hackle:	Grizzly, palmered

Cluster Midge

Hook:	#16–20 standard dry
Thread:	Black 8/0
Wings:	Grizzly hen hackle tips
Tail:	Grizzly hackle fibers
Rib:	Undersized grizzly hackle, palmered
Body:	Muskrat fur
Hackle:	Grizzly

Crane fly larva

Olive Cranefly Larva

(originator: John Barr)

Hook:	#6–10, 3XL curved shank
Weight:	15–25 turns non-lead wire
Thread:	Olive 6/0 or 8/0
Tail:	Gray marabou fluff
Rib:	3X monofilament
Shellback:	Clear Thin Skin
Body:	Olive rabbit and Antron, mixed

Tan Cranefly Larva

(originator: John Barr)

Hook:	#6–10, 3XL curved shank
Weight:	15–25 turns non-lead wire
Thread:	Tan 6/0 or 8/0
Tail:	Gray marabou fluff
Rib:	3X monofilament

Shellback: Clear Thin Skin
Body: Tan rabbit and Antron, mixed

Crane fly adult

Hewitt Skater

(originator: Edward R. Hewitt)
Hook: #14–16, 1X short dry
Thread: Unwaxed 6/0 or 8/0
Tail: None
Body: None
Hackle: Two badger spades, facing each other

Badger Spider

Hook: #12–14 standard dry
Thread: Black 8/0
Wings: Badger hackle tips
Tail: Badger hackle fibers, overlong
Body: Stripped peacock quill
Hackle: Badger, oversized

Terrestrials

Terrestrial beetles

Black Crowe Beetle

(originator: John Crowe)
Hook: #14–20 standard dry
Thread: Black 6/0 or 8/0
Shellback: Black-dyed deer hair
Body: Black thread
Legs: Butts of shellback fibers

Black Foam Beetle

Hook:	#12–22 standard dry
Thread:	Black 6/0 or 8/0
Legs:	Black-dyed deer hair
Shellback:	Black closed-cell foam
Body:	Black thread
Indicator:	Yellow poly yarn

Terrestrial ants

Black Quick-Sight Ant

Hook:	#12–22 standard dry
Thread:	Black 6/0 or 8/0
Body:	Quick-Sight foam body
Hackle:	Black, trimmed on bottom

Black Winged Ant

Hook:	#12–22 standard dry
Thread:	Black 6/0 or 8/0
Abdomen:	Black rabbit fur
Wings:	Blue dun hackle tips
Hackle:	Black, trimmed on bottom
Head:	Black rabbit fur

Grasshoppers

Parachute Hopper

(originator: Ed Schroeder)

Hook:	#6–14, 2X long
Thread:	Tan 6/0
Wing post:	White calf body hair or yellow poly yarn
Body:	Golden-tan yarn
Wing:	Mottled turkey feather section
Legs:	Pheasant tail fibers, knotted
Hackle:	Grizzly, parachute

Foam Hopper

(originator: Jim Schollmeyer)

Hook:	#12–14 short-shank dry
Thread:	Brown 6/0
Body:	Tan closed-cell foam, extended
Wing:	White poly yarn over brown poly
Legs:	Brown rubber legs
Head:	Yellow closed-cell foam

Crustaceans

Scuds

Olive Shellback Scud

Hook:	#10–16 curved scud or standard nymph
Weight:	10–15 turns non-lead wire
Thread:	Olive 6/0 or 8/0
Rib:	Working thread
Shellback:	Olive scud back or strip cut from Ziploc baggie
Body:	Olive rabbit and Antron, mixed, picked out on underside

Gray Shellback Scud

Hook:	#10–16 curved scud or standard nymph
Weight:	10–15 turns non-lead wire
Thread:	Gray 6/0 or 8/0
Rib:	Working thread
Shellback:	Gray scud back or strip cut from Ziploc baggie
Body:	Gray rabbit and Antron, mixed, picked out on underside

Aquatic sow bug

Gray Midge Nymph

Hook:	#16–20 standard nymph
Thread:	Black 8/0
Rib:	Medium copper wire
Body:	Muskrat fur dubbing

Sow Bug

Hook:	#14–18 standard nymph
Weight:	10–15 turns non-lead wire, flattened
Thread:	Gray 8/0
Tails:	Gray biots
Rib:	3X monofilament
Shellback:	Clear Thin Skin
Body:	Gray rabbit and Antron, mixed, clipped on bottom
Legs:	Body dubbing teased out to sides

Crayfish

Brown Girdle Bug

Hook:	#4–12, 3XL to 4XL
Weight:	15–25 turns non-lead wire
Thread:	Brown 6/0
Legs:	White rubber legs
Body:	Brown chenille

Clouser Crayfish

(originator: Bob Clouser)

Hook:	#4–12, 3XL
Weight:	Non-lead wire strip along each side of hook
Thread:	Tan 6/0
Antennae:	Pheasant tail fibers
Shellback:	Mottled turkey
Claws:	Hen mallard flank
Legs:	Ginger saddle hackle, palmered
Body:	Olive rabbit and Antron, mixed

Aquatic worms

Brown San Juan Worm

(originator: Chuck Rizzuto)

Hook:	#10–18 curved scud
Thread:	Tan 6/0 or 8/0
Body:	Worm brown Vernille, Ultra Chenille, or Velvet Chenille

Red San Juan Worm

(originator: Chuck Rizzuto)
Hook: #10–18 curved scud
Thread: Red 6/0 or 8/0
Body: Red Vernille, Ultra Chenille, or Velvet Chenille

Sculpin

Muddler Minnow

(originator: Dan Gapen)
Hook: #2–12, 3XL
Thread: Brown 3/0
Tail: Mottled turkey
Body: Oval gold tinsel
Underwing: Gray squirrel tail
Overwing: Mottled turkey
Collar: Deer hair
Head: Deer hair, spun and clipped

Olive Matuka Sculpin

(originator: Dave Whitlock)
Hook: #2–6, 4XL to 6XL
Weight: 15–25 turns non-lead wire
Thread: Cream 3/0
Rib: Copper wire
Body: Cream rabbit dubbing
Wing: Four olive-dyed grizzly hackles
Pectoral fins: Pheasant rump feathers
Gills: Red rabbit dubbing
Collar and head: Olive-dyed deer hair
Eyes: Green and black stick-on

22 Patterns for Stillwater Hatches

Mayflies

Speckle-Wing nymph

Pheasant Tail Flashback

Hook:	#12–18, 1XL nymph
Thread:	Brown 8/0
Tail:	Pheasant tail fibers
Rib:	Copper wire
Abdomen:	Pheasant tail fibers
Wing case:	Pearl flash
Thorax:	Peacock herl
Legs:	Pheasant tail fiber tips

Turkey Quill Callibaetis

(originator: Phil Rowley)

Hook:	#12–18, 1XL nymph
Thread:	Tan 8/0
Tail:	Tan turkey flat fiber tips
Rib:	Strand of Pearl Krystal Flash
Counter rib:	Fine gold wire
Body:	Mottled turkey fibers as herl
Wing case:	Mottled turkey feather section
Legs:	Outside wing case fibers

Speckle-Wing dun

Morris Emerger

(originator: Skip Morris)

Hook:	#12–18 curved scud
Thread:	Olive 8/0
Tail/shuck:	Brown partridge fibers
Abdomen:	Olive-tan rabbit dubbing
Thorax:	Olive-brown rabbit dubbing
Wing:	Natural deer hair

Callibaetis Compara-dun

(originators: Al Caucci and Bob Nastasi)

Hook:	#12–18 standard dry
Thread:	Olive 8/0
Wing:	Natural compara-dun deer hair
Tails:	Dun Microfibetts, split
Body:	Tan-olive Callibaetis rabbit dubbing

Speckle-Wing spinner

Speckle-Wing Quill Spinner

Hook:	#12–18 standard dry
Thread:	Gray 8/0
Tails:	Dun hackle fibers, split
Body:	Light gray–dyed hackle stem
Wings:	Grizzly hen hackle tips
Hackle:	Grizzly, trimmed top and bottom

Gulper Special

(originator: Al Troth)

Hook:	#12–18 standard dry
Thread:	Brown 8/0
Wing post:	White poly yarn
Tails:	Grizzly hackle fibers, splayed
Body:	Beaver fur
Hackle:	Grizzly, parachute

Hex nymph

Clark's Hex Emerger

(originator: Lee Clark)

Hook:	#6–12, 3XL
Head:	Gold bead
Weight:	10–20 turns non-lead wire
Thread:	Tan 6/0
Tail:	Tan marabou
Body:	Tan fur and Antron dubbing, mixed
Hackle:	Brown partridge

Hexagenia

(originator: Andy Burk)

Hook:	#6–12, 3XL curved nymph
Weight:	10–20 turns non-lead wire
Thread:	Yellow 6/0
Tail:	Gray marabou
Rib:	Copper wire
Shellback:	Turkey feather section
Gills:	Pheasant aftershaft feather
Body:	Pale yellow rabbit dubbing
Legs:	Mottled brown hen back

Hex dun

Yellow Paradrake

(originator: Mike Lawson)

Hook:	#6–8, 2X long dry fly
Thread:	Yellow 3/0 or 6/0
Wing post:	Yellow-dyed yearling elk
Hackle:	Ginger, parachute
Tail:	Moose body hairs
Body:	Yellow-dyed yearling elk, extended

Hex spinner

Big Yellow May Spinner

(originator: Polly Rosborough)

Hook:	#8, 3XL
Thread:	Tan 6/0
Tails:	Yellow and ginger hackle fibers, mixed
Body:	Yellow yarn or synthetic dubbing
Wings:	Yellow-dyed yearling elk, semi-spent
Hackle:	Yellow and ginger, mixed, V notched

Caddisflies

Cinnamon Sedge larva

Strawman

(originator: Paul Young)

Hook:	#10–14, 2XL
Thread:	Brown 6/0
Tail:	Mallard flank fibers
Body:	Deer hair, spun and clipped
Hackle:	Brown partridge

Husmask

Hook:	#10–14, 3XL
Thread:	Brown 6/0
Underbody:	Closed-cell foam
Abdomen:	Brown, grizzly, and green hackle, clipped
Thorax:	Ginger hackle, clipped
Head:	Brown rabbit dubbing

Cinnamon Sedge pupa

Ginger Deep Sparkle Pupa

(originator: Gary LaFontaine)

Hook:	#8–12, 1XL nymph
Weight:	10–20 turns non-lead wire
Thread:	Brown 6/0
Overbody:	Ginger sparkle yarn
Underbody:	Ginger Touch Dubbing
Legs:	Grouse hackle fibers
Head:	Brown rabbit and Antron, mixed

Amber Caddis Pupa

Hook:	#8–12, 1XL nymph
Weight:	8–10 turns non-lead wire
Thread:	Brown 6/0
Rib:	Amber D rib
Abdomen:	Ginger fur and sparkle yarn, mixed
Thorax and wing cases:	Ginger and brown fur and sparkle yarn mixed, picked out

Cinnamon Sedge adult

Elk Hair Caddis

(originator: Al Troth)

Hook:	#8–12 standard dry
Thread:	Tan 6/0
Hackle:	Ginger, palmered
Body:	Ginger synthetic dubbing
Wing:	Natural elk body hair

Cinnamon Sedge

Hook:	#8–12 standard dry
Thread:	Brown 6/0
Body:	Amber synthetic dubbing
Wing:	Natural deer hair
Hackle:	Brown

Traveling Sedge pupa

Olive and Brown Deep Sparkle Pupa

(originator: Gary LaFontaine)

Hook: #6–10, 1XL nymph
Weight: 15–20 turns non-lead wire
Thread: Brown 6/0
Overbody: Tan sparkle yarn
Underbody: Olive Touch Dubbing
Legs: Grouse hackle fibers
Head: Brown rabbit and Antron, mixed

Hollywood Caddis

(originator: Gordon Honey)

Hook: #6–12 curved scud
Head: Copper bead
Weight: 10–15 turns non-lead wire
Thread: Olive 6/0
Rib: Yellow floss
Abdomen: Dark olive fur and Antron, mixed
Thorax: Pheasant Tail Angel Hair

Traveling Sedge adult

Traveling Sedge Emerger

(originator: Brian Chan)

Hook: #6–12, 3XL
Thread: Olive 6/0
Rib: Bright green floss
Body: Olive seal fur
Wing: Yearling elk hair
Hackle: Brown saddle, clipped top and bottom

Mikulak Sedge

(originator: Art Mikulak)

Hook:	#6–12, 3XL curved
Thread:	Olive 6/0
Tail:	Natural elk body hair
Body:	Olive seal fur
Wings:	Natural elk in three sections
Hackle:	Brown saddle, clipped top and bottom

Midges

Midge larva

Wire Midge

Hook:	#8–20 curved scud
Thread:	Black 6/0 or 8/0
Body:	Green, red, or black wire
Head:	Black thread

Bloodworm

(originator: Brian Chan)

Hook:	#8–14, 2XL or 3XL
Thread:	Red 6/0
Tail:	Tuft of red marabou
Rib:	Copper wire
Body:	Red Super Floss
Head:	Red thread

Midge pupa

Black Beauty

(originator: Pat Dorsey)

Hook:	#14–22 curved scud
Head:	Hi-Lite silver glass bead
Thread:	Black 8/0

Rib: Silver wire
Body: Black thread
Thorax: Black rabbit dubbing

Frostbite Chironomid

(originator: Brian Chan)
Hook: #8–16 curved scud
Head: Copper bead
Thread: Black 6/0 or 8/0
Gills: White polypro yarn
Rib: Silver wire
Abdomen: Red, black, or olive Frostbite
Thorax: Peacock herl

Midge adult

CDC Midge

Hook: #16–22 standard dry
Thread: Gray 8/0 or 10/0
Body: Muskrat fur
Wing: Natural gray CDC

Ugly Duckling

(originator: Gary Anderson)
Hook: #16 extra-short shank dry
Thread: Brown 8/0
Body: Thin strip brown craft foam
Gills: White polypro yarn
Head: Orange foam

Cluster Midge

Hook: #12–20 standard dry
Thread: Black 8/0
Wings: Grizzly hen hackle tips
Tail: Grizzly hackle fibers
Rib: Undersized grizzly, palmered
Body: Muskrat fur
Hackle: Grizzly

Damselflies and dragonflies

Damselfly nymph

Baby Damsel

(originator: Brian Chan)

Hook:	#14–18 curved scud
Head:	Gold bead
Weight:	4–8 turns non-lead wire
Thread:	Olive 8/0
Tail:	Olive marabou
Rib:	Gold wire
Body:	Olive marabou, as herl

Olive Marabou Damsel

Hook:	#8–14, 3XL curved nymph
Weight:	10–15 turns non-lead wire
Thread:	Olive 6/0 or 8/0
Eyes:	Black mono eyes
Tail:	Olive marabou
Rib:	Copper wire
Body:	Olive marabou, as herl
Wing case:	Olive marabou
Thorax:	Olive rabbit dubbing

Damselfly adult

Foam Teneral Damsel

(originator: Phil Rowley)

Hook:	#10–12 standard dry
Thread:	Black 8/0
Body:	Round foam, olive
Wings:	Pearlescent sheet, 1/8" width
Thorax:	Olive-dyed deer hair, spun and clipped
Eyes:	Round foam, black

Blue Damsel Adult

(originator: Andy Burke)

Hook:	#10–12 standard dry
Thread:	Blue Monocord
Abdomen:	Blue Z-Lon or Damsel body, furled
Wings:	Dun hackle tips
Thorax:	Blue-dyed deer hair, spun and clipped
Legs:	Blue Monocord
Eyes:	Black mono eyes

Dragonfly nymph

Beaverpelt

(originator: Don Earnest)

Hook:	#4–12, 3XL curved nymph
Weight:	15–20 turns non-lead wire
Thread:	Olive 6/0
Body:	Olive-dyed beaver or similar dubbing
Hackle:	Pheasant rump
Head:	Olive dyed beaver or similar dubbing

Predator

(originator: Skip Morris)

Hook:	#6–12, 2XL or 3XL
Thread:	Brown 3/0
Overbody:	Brown 1/16" foam
Underbody:	Olive rabbit dubbing
Eyes:	Black mono eyes
Legs:	Brown or speckled rubber legs

Water boatman

Stillwater Boatman

(originator: Gary Anderson)

Hook:	#14–20 standard nymph
Weight or flotation:	4–6 turns weight or foam
Thread:	Olive 8/0
Legs:	Black rubber legs
Body:	Peacock herl

Boatman

(originator: Jim Schollmeyer)

Hook:	#10–16 standard nymph
Weight:	10–12 turns non-lead wire, flattened
Thread:	Olive 8/0
Eyes:	Black mono eyes
Shellback:	Black Thin Skin
Air bubble:	Clear sparkle yarn
Body:	Olive sparkle yarn
Legs:	Olive goose biots

Alderfly adult

Alderfly

(originator: Charles Kingsley)

Hook:	#10–14 standard wet
Thread:	Black 6/0 or 8/0
Rib:	Oval gold tinsel
Body:	Peacock herl
Hackle:	Black hen
Wing:	Dark turkey feather sections

Scud

Olive Beadhead Scud

Hook:	#10–16, 1XL nymph
Head:	Gold bead

Weight:	10–15 turns non-lead wire
Thread:	Olive 6/0 or 8/0
Rib:	3X monofilament
Shellback:	Olive Scud Back
Body:	Olive rabbit dubbing with red egg sac

Olive Fast-Sinking Scud

(originator: Rich Osthoff)

Hook:	#10–16, 1XL nymph
Weight:	15–25 turns non-lead wire
Thread:	Olive 6/0 or 8/0
Tail:	Hen pheasant breast fibers
Shellback:	Clear Scud back
Back stripe:	Silver Mylar tinsel
Underbody:	Olive yarn
Rib:	3X to 5X monofilament
Body:	Olive rabbit and sparkle yarn, mixed

Leech

Beadhead Black Woolly Bugger

(Russell Blessing)

Hook:	#6–14, 3XL
Head:	Gold bead
Weight:	10–20 turns non-lead wire
Thread:	Black 6/0 or 8/0
Tail:	Black marabou with 6–8 strands pearl flash
Body:	Black chenille
Hackle:	Black hen

Black Bunny Leech

Hook:	#4–12, 4XL to 6XL
Head:	Black tungsten bead
Weight:	15–20 turns non-lead wire
Thread:	Black 3/0 or 6/0
Tail:	Black rabbit strip with red flash
Body:	Black rabbit strip, wound

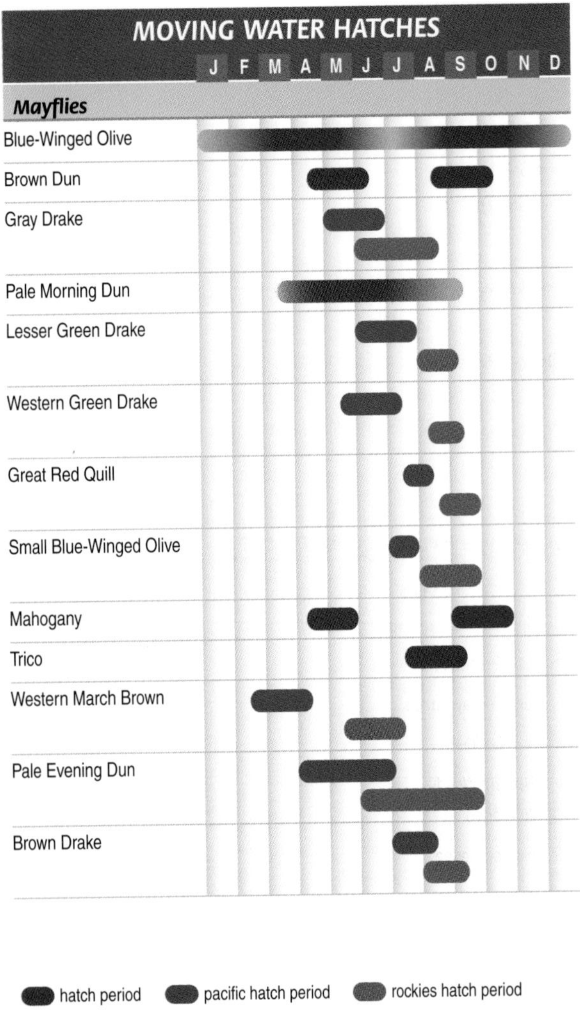
MOVING WATER HATCHES
J F M A M J J A S O N D
Mayflies
Blue-Winged Olive
Brown Dun
Gray Drake
Pale Morning Dun
Lesser Green Drake
Western Green Drake
Great Red Quill
Small Blue-Winged Olive
Mahogany
Trico
Western March Brown
Pale Evening Dun
Brown Drake
hatch period
pacific hatch period
rockies hatch period

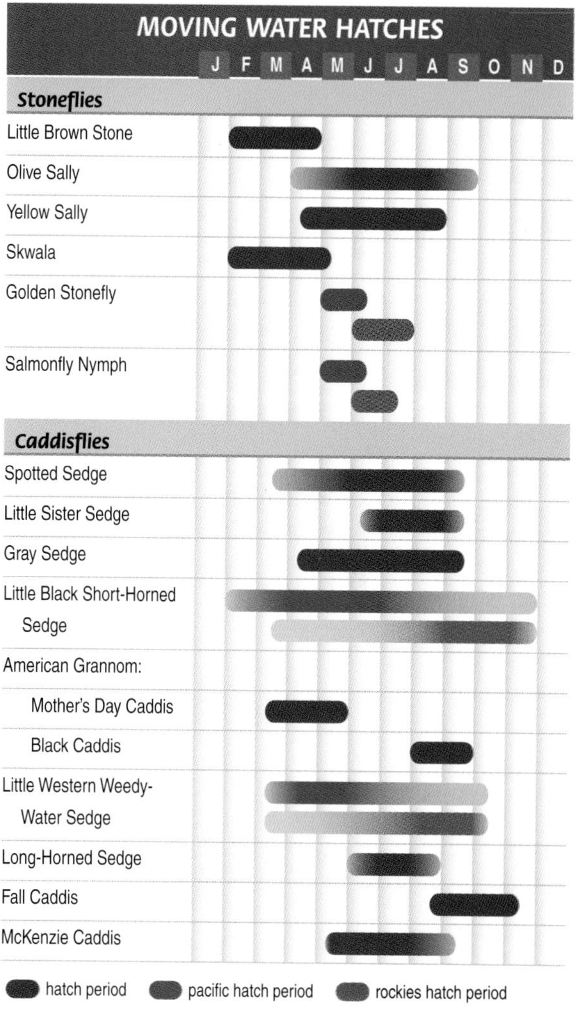
MOVING WATER HATCHES
J F M A M J J A S O N D
Stoneflies
Little Brown Stone
Olive Sally
Yellow Sally
Skwala
Golden Stonefly
Salmonfly Nymph
Caddisflies
Spotted Sedge
Little Sister Sedge
Gray Sedge
Little Black Short-Horned Sedge
American Grannom:
Mother's Day Caddis
Black Caddis
Little Western Weedy-Water Sedge
Long-Horned Sedge
Fall Caddis
McKenzie Caddis
hatch period
pacific hatch period
rockies hatch period

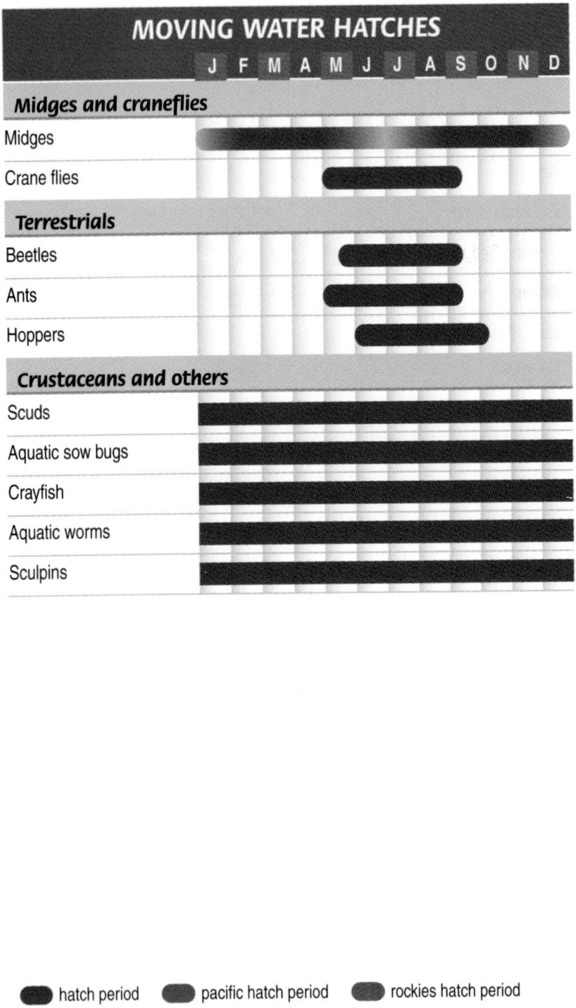
MOVING WATER HATCHES
J F M A M J J A S O N D
Midges and craneflies
Midges
Crane flies
Terrestrials
Beetles
Ants
Hoppers
Crustaceans and others
Scuds
Aquatic sow bugs
Crayfish
Aquatic worms
Sculpins
hatch period
pacific hatch period
rockies hatch period

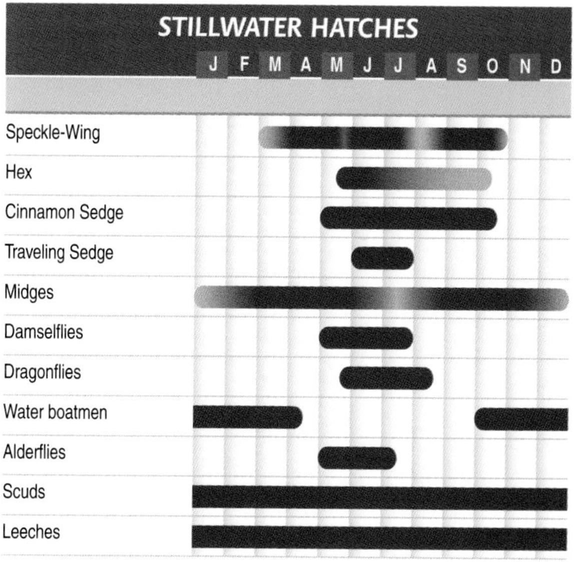
STILLWATER HATCHES
J F M A M J J A S O N D
Speckle-Wing
Hex
Cinnamon Sedge
Traveling Sedge
Midges
Damselflies
Dragonflies
Water boatmen
Alderflies
Scuds
Leeches

hatch period
pacific hatch period
rockies hatch period

Index

Page numbers in *italics* indicate illustrations and page numbers in **bold** indicate detailed descriptions.